WOODBINE WILLIE

An Anglican Incident
Being some account of the life and times
of
Geoffrey Anketell Studdert Kennedy
poet, prophet, seeker after truth, 1883 - 1929

By

WILLIAM PURCELL

The prophet is a fool, the spiritual man is mad

Hosea 9 : 7

HODDER AND STOUGHTON

ACKNOWLEDGEMENTS

Acknowledgement is made to the following publishers for their kind permission to quote from their publications: Chatto and Windus Ltd., Faber and Faber Ltd., J. M. Dent & Sons Ltd., John Murray, A. R. Mowbray & Co., and Wm. Collins & Sons.

Copyright © 1962 by William Purcell
First Printed 1962
Abridged edition (reset) 1965

PRINTED IN GREAT BRITAIN FOR HODDER AND STOUGHTON LIMITED, ST. PAUL'S HOUSE, WARWICK LANE, LONDON, E.C.4 BY C. TINLING AND CO. LIMITED, LIVERPOOL, LONDON AND PRESCOT

To

THE RT. REV.
CUTHBERT KILLICK NORMAN BARDSLEY

Bishop of Coventry
Pastor, Prophet, Evangelist
with respect and affection

CONTENTS

An Industrious Christian Fellow

FOREWORD

"NOT enough has been written about this great and good man." Such was the opinion of Geoffrey Studdert Kennedy's contemporary, 'Dick' Sheppard, writing in *The Times* just after his friend's death in 1929. A few months later, however, in the book *G. A. Studdert Kennedy: By His Friends*, seven men who had known and loved him—they included Sheppard himself, as well as William Temple—collected together some personal reminiscences—a symposium which has been of much value to the making of this book. From then until now, that has been all, and the memory of one of the most appealing figures of his day and age has been almost totally lost. This present book represents an attempt at re-discovery.

The endeavour has certainly proved the accuracy of the opinion expressed by another of Studdert Kennedy's friends, P. T. R. Kirk, sometime General Director of the Industrial Christian Fellowship, that "the story of his life will not be a simple thing to tell". Chief among the reasons for this has been the fact that Studdert Kennedy, in his profound humility, was the last person in the world to consider himself as of sufficient importance to warrant documentation. The result was that, in terms of personal memorabilia, he left very little behind. And since his appeal lay always as much in what he was, as in what he said or did, personal memories of him, not always easy to obtain at this distance of time, have been of exceptional importance to the attempt to form some kind of picture of him.

There have been many, however, who have been generous with help, and among those I would like particularly to thank: Mrs. Emily Studdert Kennedy and The Rev. H. G. Studdert Kennedy.

All those others who have also been generous with their time in assisting, in various ways, this present writer in his inquiries will perhaps take this brief word as a nonetheless warmly felt expression of his gratitude.

Perhaps it should be added that, in so far as this present book touches upon the Industrial Christian Fellowship, it does so with reference only to the early years of that still happily continuing body when G.S.K. was connected therewith, and makes no claim to being in any sense a history of it.

This book is the record of a man and his work and as such has not been concerned in any way with his personal and domestic life. This is as his family requested. But it will become clear that the man and his work would not have been possible except at the cost of considerable sacrifice, on the part of both Geoffrey Studdert Kennedy and his wife, of their personal and family life. This cost they willingly faced together as part of the price which God demands of those who share a prophet's calling. But perhaps it will not be out of place to express appreciation of Mrs. Studdert Kennedy's unobtrusive share in this "Anglican Incident".

WILLIAM PURCELL

CHAPTER I

THE HOUSE IN LEEDS

TOWARDS the middle of the bitter winter of 1915–16 a very new chaplain arrived in France. Soon afterwards he was to be met, at most hours of the day and night, in a large and noisy shed on the *Rive Gauche* railway siding in the town of Rouen. The shed was a canteen, in which drafts for the front, having come up from Le Havre, could pause awhile before moving on a further stage towards what, in that old war, was likely to be fairly rapid extinction for the majority.

The new chaplain, in his own odd way, was something of a success, foreshadowing the enormous fame which was later to be his. To the Assistant Chaplain General he had mentioned, as qualification for the job of spiritual ministration in the canteen, that he was once "a revolutionary agnostic socialist who used to stand on a tub and talk in public places in the Midlands". It soon became his routine to stand on a box and announce to the crowds of soldiery that he was about to sing: *Mother Machree* for the sons, *Little Grey Home in the West* for the husbands, *The Sunshine of Your Smile* for the lovers. Afterwards he would offer to write home for them, and was to be seen doing so, surrounded by a throng pressing in on him. And, when the time came for them to go, he would be by the train as it pulled out until he was left, heavy with his thoughts, to watch its vanishing tail-light.

He was thirty-two. He had bat-wing ears; his mouth gave the impression of being over large for its surroundings, and the man himself appeared astonished at the fact of his being rigged out in the officer's uniform of the day; Captain's pips at cuff and shoulder, the Maltese cross of a padre in cap and lapels. He wore it untidily. There were occasions later when the untidiness merged into disarray, as when he was discovered wearing immense spurs, one of them upside down.

The new chaplain's name was Geoffrey Anketell Studdert Kennedy, a man destined within a year or so to become known as Woodbine Willie, legendary padre of the first world war. He was also fated to rise in reputation, like a Verey light, above the smoke of it; to hang in the sky, a portent and a prophecy, for ten years afterwards, and then to decline earthwards into darkness again. But he left a glow, and it will be that glow which will concern us in this story, because it is very precious. It is the glow of Christ-like love and understanding combined with an immense ability to make God understood in a world in which, as a person, as a power, as a presence to make Everyman open his soul as a daisy to the sun, he appears sometimes to be dead.

His story begins in a vicarage in a poor district of Leeds, in the eighties of the last century, the garden of which was encompassed by a workhouse, a board school, a brick quarry, and a pub known as the Cemetery Tavern. The area was dirty, a region of courts gas-lit, doubtful by night. There were those, indeed, who claimed Quarry Hill, Leeds, to be one of the worst slums in the North. There, suitably enough, Geoffrey Anketell Studdert Kennedy was born.

But now the house has vanished. So has most of the district, as once it was, which is no doubt just as well, slum clearance having made spaces where once the courts clustered. So also have gone almost all of the family into which, in the vicarage, on June 27th, 1883, Geoffrey was born. But the church of St. Mary's still stands, that church, with which, for many years, the lives of the Studdert Kennedy's were bound up.

In this church, in a side chapel, behind a curtain, there is a tablet, one of four in a building bare as a hangar. It has this to say:

This Chapel dedicated to the Holy Child
was fitted and furnished for divine service
by the congregation and friends of St. Mary's Church
to the glory of God and in affectionate memory of Joan
wife of the Reverend William Studdert Kennedy,
Vicar of this parish. A good example to us all during
thirty years as wife, mother, and friend.

A.D. 1913

This is the woman who lay in childbed over at the now vanished vicarage on the 27th day of June, 1883. For her, it was a familiar experience. There had been six babies before this one, and there were to be two more. For her husband, also, such occasions were by no means novel, since there had been five children of his first marriage.

William Studdert Kennedy, second son of the Very Reverend R. M. Kennedy, Dean of Clonfert, and Anne Studdert of County Clare, was an Irishman.

Fifty-eight at this seventh baby's birth, he had begun his ministry as curate of Ballymena. He became Rector of St. Doulough's, Malahide, Dublin, and there stayed for fourteen years. After that, like so many of his kind, he crossed the Irish Sea and for a further fourteen years was Vicar of Shires Head, Garstang, in Lancashire. And then, in 1876, he was instituted to St. Mary's, Quarry Hill, Leeds, brick kiln, Cemetery Tavern, Workhouse and all. He remained there thirty-seven years, until his death in 1914.

By his first wife, a Miss Russell of Malahide, there had been Mabel, Norah, Eve, Francis and John Russell

Kennedy, later to be head of the Far Eastern Section of the Associated Press in Tokyo.

And then his wife died. The widower, perplexed as to the future of his young family, after a suitable interval sought a second. He found her in an eighteen-year-old girl, Joan Anketell of County Clare. She was his partner for forty-one years, an understanding person whose energies and interests, not surprisingly, found more than enough to absorb them in bringing up so large a family.

The Vicar of Quarry Hill was a quiet man, not easily separated from, nor often found out of, his parish. He could be persuaded to a concert in Leeds, of which there were many in that musical city, only if his wife were singing, which she often did. But, for the most part, to stay in his parish, to support any Liberal in politics, and the nationalism of John Redmond, represented the limit of his ambitions. He had, however, one aversion, and that was for doctors. He maintained, with the confidence of one whose own health was perfect, that "they made people sick by making them sick-minded". Christian Science came in time to claim the allegiance of several of the family, so that the Church of their baptism knew them no more, and that of Mrs. Eddy claimed them for its own. Indeed, there was a time when it almost claimed Geoffrey himself, in which case the Church of England would have lost a prophet and that of Christ Scientist gained, maybe, another practitioner. But how far this development was due, ultimately and unconsciously, to the aversion of the vicar to doctors it is impossible to know.

Yet all this was very far in the future when the new baby arrived on that June day of 1883. What sort of a child was he?

When a storm shrieked over Leeds one night in his

second year, it brought down a chimney in the vicarage at Quarry Hill. The debris fell by the cot; but when the child was brought out of the wreckage he was observed to be still smiling broadly. When he was seven the asthma which shadowed him through life struck for the first time and it was remembered how, as the boy lay wheezing, his very large, hurt brown eyes seemed to become more noticeable than ever. And a little later the braying laughter of the same child, as he stood with others round a nigger minstrel show, so grated upon one of the performers that he turned to him with the remark: "My lad, you have a horrid laugh." Thus the man of the years to come was seen, or thought to have been seen, in the child. That combination of the gallant, the pathetic and the ridiculous many found, in after times, to be not the least among the many oddities of the man which so strangely touched the heart.

There were other characteristics which early emerged in him. One was absent-mindedness. His excuse was usually that 'he was thinking of something different', as on the occasion when, sent to order two pounds of strawberries and a stone of potatoes, he caused to be delivered two stones of strawberries and one pound of potatoes. Such, at any rate, was for long a family tradition, just as a family memory was of the dismay of the boy when he discovered, as often happened, the inconvenience his forgetting had occasioned. But the cause of this dreamy detachment was plain enough. He was a reader, as insatiable as unselective. Any print seemed to fascinate him, and the man who in later years could become in a train so lost in a book as to forget even his whereabouts and the nature of his journey was foreshadowed in the boy to whom reading was from the first a passion. The matter is of importance. He was often judged in later times to be a shallow thinker who made up by showmanship what he lacked in depth. That was never true. The showmanship may well have existed. Indeed, it was the means by which his message was communicated. But the message was there. That he was a voice, and of other things nothing, could never with any justice be said of him, even though it was in fact often said.

He was educated at a private school, run by a Mr. Knightley, at Leeds Grammar School, and at Trinity College, Dublin.

Geoffrey was happy at Leeds Grammar School. And it says a good deal for the civilised nature of the place that his almost theatrical Irishness caused little friction. No one could mistake that upper lip : and if they did the accent would have put them right. That was something he always tended to overdo. A fellow student at the Ripon Clergy School in after years exclaimed, "I wish Kennedy wouldn't speak like a Dublin jarvie to show he's an Irishman!" But Kennedy did, and in times to come many thousands of people, including captains and kings of his day and age, heard him doing so, not always with approval.

At the end of 1902 Geoffrey left school to take the T.C.D. third year examinations. He gained a Junior Moderatorship and Silver Medal in Classics. And then at the close of the academic year of 1904 he completed his degree at Trinity College, Dublin, after a final furious burst of work. He was twenty-one. It was time for him to go out into the world.

He turned to teaching. The Grammar School whose staff he joined in the January of 1905 was at Caldey Grange, in Cheshire. He was there two and a half years, happily teaching general subjects, outwardly content enough, yet inwardly stirring with the pressure of new ideas.

In any event, the time was one for experiment. Already a very large gap in outlook and ideas had appeared between people of William Studdert Kennedy's generation and that of his children. Maybe this tempo of the times, with its emphasis on change in a new century, had some connection with the turning to Christian Science of so many of the family. It was certainly true that the period abounded in new creeds as a cactus-house with peculiar shapes. Theosophy and Mrs. Besant were to be encountered; reincarnation was discussed as a matter of some moment; and the grisly hand of spiritualism was watched by some with breathless interest as it groped at the veil held to shroud the Beyond. Everything, to those who thought at all, and were young enough, seemed in a state of flux, and this spirit of the times bore with particular force upon the whole field of belief.

Such were some of the ideas frothily afloat on the surface of some lives at that time. They seemed important; but the sad hindsight of history reveals them as trivial compared to the sombre undetected fact that the pace of the whole fateful stream which bore them along was quickening as it approached the Niagara of the catastrophe which was to come. That catastrophe, of course, engulfed them all, including Geoffrey, and those who survived to surface again in the post-war whirlpool at the foot of it were different people, in a different world. That is part of Geoffrey's story, too, as we shall see.

Meanwhile, for him, in his early twenties, the years of teaching at Caldey Grange were happy enough, a period of vigorous, disordered reading, an extension into adult life of the habit of childhood. Each new idea as it came along possessed his attention wholly, with the result that he tended to be taken with a series of notions as they came along. He was an enthusiast, then, as always. And whether the current enthusiasm were for a commentary on Isaiah, or for some work on varieties of sexual behaviour, made little difference to the zest with which he would talk of it. And then, in the October of 1907, Geoffrey abandoned schoolmastering to enter Ripon Clergy College.

He was there from October 1907 to the June of the following year, a very short time by modern standards in such matters. Then in the summer of 1908, in the Cathedral at Worcester, he was ordained deacon, and went thence to Rugby Parish Church, where his brother had been before him.

The new curate dropped upon the parish like a bomb, making a small crater in its collective memory, the outlines of which can even still faintly be made out. The lodging where Geoffrey had his bed-sitting room has gone : the slum area in which, before he had been there long, the children used to follow him as though he were the Pied Piper in a cassock, has vanished away. But the memory of the extraordinary character who came upon them persisted in Rugby for a long time afterwards.

In one thing at this time, Geoffrey was extremely fortunate—the character of the then Rector of Rugby, A. V. Baillie, godson of Queen Victoria, a nephew of Dean Stanley, and subsequently for many years Dean of Windsor.

It was an interesting time to arrive in Rugby, since the whole place was going through a phase of radical change. Indeed, the situation in Rugby in those days merits a closer look, since it illustrates clearly an abiding truth about the English social scene—that behind an outward face of the ordinary lurks an inner life—usually understood only by the natives and guarded by them as an esoteric secret—of the most extraordinary complexity.

Thus to the outward view the Rugby upon which Geoffrey descended was a plain-faced town of uninspiring aspect. In the middle of it stood Rugby School. Nearby was the parish church, completed in the nineties. Opposite the church was the market square; on the outskirts was the great railway centre. And, springing from this, the factories of heavy industry were making their appearance. The result was a variegated community in which the social classes could be discerned as clearly as the layers in a cake.

At the top came the professional classes; beneath them the established tradesmen, then the railwaymen. The outsiders were the industrial workers. There were also further complications. The old market town of Tom Brown's Schooldays, pre-railway, and long pre-industrial, was a centre for hunting and, of all things, polo, so that there were still men to be found in it who could say, as one groom did shortly after Baillie's arrival: "Very nice gentleman, the new Rector—a good rider, with fine hands." The opinion this shrewd Rector formed of his curate is interesting.

"K. was one of the strangest characters I ever knew. An Irishman, with brains, he had infinite charm, complete devotion to his work, and a fine sense of humour. But mentally he was incredibly undisciplined. At least once a week he dashed into my room with some new idea. They were sometimes quite preposterous; but they were always held by him with burning earnestness. If one argued with him gravely about them, he was quite clever enough to have defended his position with success, when the result would only have been to harden his beliefs. But his new idea always had a humorous side due to its very exaggeration, and an appeal to that brought him down on his feet again.

"In his earlier days he preached a sermon in the

heat of the moment in which I felt he had gone more than a little too far. After church I took him for a walk in the Rectory garden and, with apparent gravity, I said, 'You know, I think you exaggerated when you said there had been no one between yourself and St. Paul who had understood the Gospel'. At once he burst into a shout of uproarious laughter. He had learnt his lesson. I always told him he must not come to me with more than one heresy a week, as after that it became a bore."[1]

This was leadership of genius. It is difficult to think of any other kind of guidance, so patient, humorous and wise, which could more effectively, or at all, have held Geoffrey on even an approximately even keel. And since the result was to preserve him for the Church as a burning and a shining light it is possible to feel some little gratitude, even at this distance of time.

"K. had no sort of discipline about small things," Baillie recorded, "what he had in his pocket he gave away, until his landlady took charge of his money and rationed him with it. It was the same with his clothes. He gave them all away and walked about almost in rags, wearing a cassock to conceal the fact."[2] Baillie does not record, however, that the landlady in question, a good soul by the name of Miss Moore, having in pity bought him an overcoat, was not unnaturally incensed when he immediately gave it away. The overcoat was not replaced. Quixotic generosity, however appealing, is not always easy to live with. It can sometimes be a pose, though with Geoffrey it seems, by the test of continuance, to have been natural enough. The extreme open-handedness continued throughout his life, so did the sartorial eccentricity.

[1] A. V. Baillie: *My First Eighty Years*.
[2] ibid.

20

Twenty years after these early days in Rugby, when he was a national figure, there was an occasion when he set off for an important occasion in Westminster Abbey wearing football shorts under the scarlet robes of a royal chaplain. Even then it was necessary for him to return hurriedly to the vicarage of Christ Church, Westminster, where he was then staying, because he had forgotten his teeth.

Baillie is clear, however, on one important fact — that the new curate, all oddities notwithstanding, was a remarkable man. "His complete sincerity," he wrote, "his passionate belief and astonishing eloquence made him a great power for good in my Rugby parish. We had one small district that was practically a slum, and K. gravitated there, getting me to buy a derelict Noncomformist Chapel as the centre for his work. His work was very useful. One of his activities was to wander in and out of the pubs and talk to the men. His personality made it easy, and the men would welcome him even in the worst and lowest places."[1]

Here, already, then, in Rugby, the twin characteristics which distinguished his life to the end were already visible: the eloquence and the deep love of the poor. As to the first, it was not long before masters of Rugby School formed the habit of going to hear him whenever they knew he was to be in the pulpit. Herbert, sometime Bishop of Blackburn and Norwich, who was a fellow-curate at Rugby, recalled of that preaching:

"There must be few men of whom it is true, as it was of him, that from the moment of his ordination he was really miserable if he were not allowed to preach at least twice a Sunday. There was so much he wanted to say, so many thoughts bobbing up in his mind, that silence was a severe discipline. As to the

[1] ibid.

21

matter and manner of his preaching, clear impressions will remain for all who heard him. A sermon on the Holy Communion, tracing the universal power of that sacred bread and wine, through all ages and amongst all sort of people, which the listener suddenly realised to be a sermon entirely in blank verse; or again a Good Friday sermon on the meaning of the Atonement which made a somewhat complacent congregation think as it had seldom thought before : or the simple mission addresses to his own special congregation of tramps and lodging-house inmates—these were indications of his mind that those who heard him will not forget."[1]

And as to the second characteristic here to be seen emerging, that love of the poor, the word 'gravitated' used by Baillie is significant. Geoffrey gravitated towards the slum area of the parish as a compass swings to the north because it was a built-in disposition of his to do so. It was part of the man. He was genuinely at home amid the smell of poverty, the doss-house mutterings, and the pitiful anxieties of want. Some people —and they have included some of the most high-principled possessors of the social conscience—have entered this shadow world of burst boots and pieces of food wrapped in newspaper out of a sense of duty. Geoffrey belonged to the much smaller number of those who go there, not because they think they ought to, so much as because they really want to. He was glad when they said unto him that he had to go into the house of the poor. That was where he belonged.

"I can see again," Herbert wrote, "that small slim figure strolling into the unattractive pub where his beloved lodging-house tramps were to be found, and standing up to the bar in his cassock to sing 'Nazareth', while half his audience 'felt within a power

[1] *G. A. Studdert Kennedy: By His Friends.*

unfelt before'. They loved him—loved him for his great laugh, the smile that transformed his face, the Irish brogue, but most of all because of his love for them. He was entirely at home in the dirtiest of kitchens, and would sit for hours smoking and talking, or watching by a sick-bed, forgetting, in all probability some important engagement elsewhere. This was sometimes a source of trouble: he was known on more than one occasion to start off to take a funeral at the cemetery and then, dropping in on someone on the way, to forget all about it."[1]

There was another fellow-curate of Geoffrey's at Rugby, Selwyn Bean, later Archdeacon of Manchester, who was personally involved in some of the consequences of this forgetfulness.

"In those days, Rugby with its five churches, the Hospital Chapel and the Workhouse Chapel, meant careful planning and organisation. If this was to be properly carried out it was necessary for each member of the staff to be at the right place at the right time. K. found this one of the most difficult tasks to carry out. Each curate in turn was responsible for a week's duty. This meant that the man on duty was responsible, among other things, for funerals for which no special arrangements had been made. My lodgings were quite close to the cemetery, and I well remember one week, in which K. was on duty, I was sent for early on Tuesday afternoon, before I set out visiting, to take a funeral which was waiting at the cemetery gate. I rushed round to the cemetery, robed, and took the funeral. Exactly the same thing happened on the following Friday and I was a little disconcerted when I hurried to the cemetery to hear one of the onlookers say that is the second funeral I had forgotten that week! I felt it was only fair to mention it at the

[1] ibid.

staff meeting on the Monday morning. K. was very penitent and said that he would try very hard not to forget a funeral again. In those days death certificates were printed on blue paper and the parish clerk would put the day and time of the funeral on the death certificate and leave it at the lodgings of the curate who was on duty. Some weeks later, I met K. in the Market Place of Rugby and he had stuck in his button-hole what looked like a blue spill of paper. I jokingly asked him if he had joined the blue riband brigade. His reply was typical—'No, I have got a funeral this afternoon and I'm trying to remember it.'

"Within a stone's-throw of the parish church there was a small slum area, which disappeared years ago. But in 1910, it consisted of three or four very rough lodging-houses and a number of houses and cottages which were hardly fit for human occupation. On the edge of this area, stood the Parish Hall. The Rector put K. in charge of this district. Here every Sunday evening he held a mission service, and the way in which he gathered his congregation from lodging-houses and slums was indeed remarkable. There was something irresistible about K. and they loved him. I always remember one old woman in that district who, when she was dying, sent for K., and after he had said some prayers said, 'Now sing me the *Mountains of Mourne*', and K. with his wonderful voice sang as she passed away.

"During his short time at Rugby, he already showed signs of that amazing gift for preaching, which made him so well known in later years. But it is true to say that his style, and indeed his matter, did not appeal to some of the ladies who formed the weekday Even-song congregation at Holy Trinity. It was the custom at the beginning of the year for one of the curates to preach at the Choral Evensong on each Saints Day. I well remember on one occasion when I was taking the service on the Feast of St. Simon and St. Jude. K., startled and almost horrified his congregation by the opening words of his sermon in which he stated the Epistle of St. Jude was the most repulsive document in the New Testament. One of the maiden ladies of the congregation wrote to the Rector afterwards and complained. On another occasion in the same Church of Holy Trinity, in which many of the stained glass windows had been placed in memory of the friends and relations of members of the congregation. K., during the course of the sermon on the reality of religion somewhat distressed many people by saying there were times when he would like to take a great sledge-hammer, smash every stained glass window in this church and go out and celebrate the Lord's Supper in the fields with a cup and platter."[1]

Baillie attached his new curate to Holy Trinity, Rugby, and from there his work among the poor branched out. It also invaded the lodging which he had with the long-suffering Miss Moore, she who bought him the overcoat. The house, in a street leading from the Market Place to the main gate of Rugby School, was full of narrow passages. Most of its rooms were small; but there was one of some size. This was soon converted into a playroom for the children of Sun Street nearby, most of them barefooted, after the habit of the day. Sun Street, in fact —perhaps so called because it was usually in shadow —was the scene of Geoffrey's most typical work in Rugby. For the small children chiefly of this region he invented the Babies' Service, where the congregation on a Sunday afternoon would be composed entirely of such, with Geoffrey in the middle of them, telling stories, having them sing verses, helping

[1] Privately communicated.

them light birthday candles. There are not many men, as opposed to women, of whom such a story could be told without a certain queasiness. Yet no one seems to have found any of it odd in Geoffrey. No doubt the Babies' Service was crude sentiment. But he was a crudely sentimental person, which is a valuable asset when working among the Sun Streets of this world. Moreover, Geoffrey's sentimentality, as represented especially in some of his war poems, was of a characteristically proletarian variety, where 'you' tends to rhyme with 'thru' and all emotions are a little larger than life, like the porcelain flowers under a glass dome on a sooty Edwardian grave labelled 'Mum'. A slum priest who could quite naturally revel in this sort of thing himself would by that fact be well on the way towards the hearts of his people. With Geoffrey, this innate sentimentality was magnetic to simple folk whether their slum happened to be Sun Court, Rugby; a trench in the France of the first world war, or a dole queue afterwards. The same disposition enabled him, a little later, when he had a parish in Worcester, to make such a thing of funerals, where it was not uncommon for all concerned, including the officiant, to be bathed in tears.

Yet with Geoffrey this sentimentality did not, as it so often does, go with simplicity. He was no fool. The masters from Rugby School did not go to hear him because he talked nonsense, but because what he said had power. Nonetheless, his marked sentimentality and intellectual ability made a curious combination. Perhaps the verdict of his fellow-curate Herbert approaches as close as possible to an explanation of it:

". . . He was entirely unacademic. Not only was his mind out of tune with a purely scholastic atmosphere; but it was impossible for him to disassociate his thoughts of God from his love for men. For him

26

the setting and the stage of religion was this world, and his own intense humaneness kept his intellectual side harnessed, if not subordinate, to his pastoral work."[1]

He was happy at Rugby, though he was certainly not treated with undue indulgence. Another of Baillie's admirable customs was to welcome his curates to his house on Sunday evenings and to command them, in a body, to his study on Monday mornings, when the duties of the week would be discussed and allocated. The body so assembled contained a high proportion of able men; Herbert and Askwith were future bishops of Norwich and Gloucester; Julian Bickersteth a future headmaster of a famous Australian school and Canon of Canterbury. These among others were not the kind of men likely to accept the dogmatisms of an excitable junior without reply. So there were frequent disputations among the young men in each others' rooms, often, as Herbert remembered, with Geoffrey walking up and down the carpet, violently destroying all arguments brought against his current viewpoint, then as suddenly, and with a wide smile, admitting he was wrong. So he was kept in order, given due scope to follow his own various bents, and surrounded by friendship. That indeed was the environment which his particular kind of personality, at once singularly warm-hearted yet also liable to hurt, needed beyond all else.

It continued four years, during which, after a two years diaconate, he was ordained priest. It might have been prolonged considerably. The Edwardian curate not of officer class often stayed as he was for a very long time. As it happened, however, events were taking place back in his father's parish at Quarry Hill, Leeds, which seemed to Geoffrey to call for his return to the place of his birth.

All was not well there. By 1912 William Studdert

[1] *G. A. Studdert Kennedy: By His Friends.*

Kennedy had been Vicar of St. Mary's, Quarry Hill, thirty-five years, and was eighty-seven himself, a survivor from a vanishing world. Even by the time of his arrival at Quarry Hill in the eighties the great old parish church of Leeds nearby — 't'owd church', as it was known — had far overshadowed its humbler neighbour, and as time passed this became more marked. Even in Geoffrey's boyhood, St. Mary's could hardly have been called flourishing. But now, with the new century, had come other influences to change noticeably the whole character of the area. The clothing trade of Leeds had brought in many German Jews, a large number of whom had settled in the parish, and the old vicar could but note sadly the replacement of the Leeds folk he had lived among for so many years by these newcomers. So St. Mary's by 1912 was a run-down church, and its vicar was a very old widower.

There then came another event, like one of the ill-tidings in the Book of Job, to trouble his old age. Cecil, younger brother to Geoffrey, was to go the whole way with the Church of Christ Scientist, ultimately becoming a Christian Science practitioner in Victoria, Vancouver. That was the point at which Geoffrey left Rugby to return to Leeds.

He went to be curate in the place of his brother. Rather curiously, however, there arose some difficulty with authority, which apparently did not approve, except on the condition that Geoffrey should regard himself as on the staff of the neighbouring Parish Church. There, as one of twelve other curates, he would be under the surveillance of the Vicar of Leeds, Dr. Bickersteth. The arrangement worked well enough and for the next two years, until the death of his father in 1914, he was in Leeds again. His position was a curious one; at once on the staff of the parish church and not fully of it, since his first loyalty was to his father in the vicarage at Quarry Hill. There at St. Mary's, run down as the place was, Geoffrey's coming brought a rapid change for the better. Even to that unlikely area he began to attract even from a distance, so that people began to make their way to hear him as the masters at Rugby School had once done.

Sometimes, too, he went further afield. He was beginning to be heard of. Thus in November 1913, when a mission was to be held in Barrow-in-Furness and last-minute difficulties over a missioner had arisen, someone recalled hearing of an extraordinary young curate working with his aged father in a slum parish in Leeds. Not without doubts, he was sent for. The doubts were deepened by his appearance. He arrived in glossy black clothes and an astonishingly, a truly remarkable silk hat from which it was difficult to avert the eye. Clearly very young, very Irish and very shy, he was not inspiring. But all doubts vanished when he gave his first address. One who was there, and recalled the occasion many years later, remembered the startling impact of the torrent of words in manner and meaning so unusual, upon those who heard it. And then, as suddenly as he had arrived, he left, having to produce a play, he shyly explained, back in his father's parish. The man who thus encountered him, a fellow-missioner at Barrow, scarcely ever met him again. But as the years passed, and he heard of the fame of the little Irishman, he was not surprised.[1]

Even so, it was probably a good thing that he had the steadying influence and the good fellowship of the parish church at Leeds behind him at this stage. There is a glimpse of an anglican era vanished forever

[1] *Church Times*, March 15th, 1929.

in the picture of Friday lunch-times in Leeds Vicarage in these years, when no less than a full dozen of curates—for such was the size of the staff in those opulent days—gathered for their weekly meeting, followed by lunch and billiards. Geoffrey would be with them, and often afterwards he would stay to discuss with Bickersteth his own particular problems at St. Mary's. It would have surprised that good man, as it would indeed have astounded anybody, to know that within seven years at the most the large-eyed, Irish curate anxiously discussing the affairs of the neighbouring parish with him would be a national figure.

In his private life there now came to Geoffrey a development of the utmost importance. He fell in love, and became engaged to be married. Emily Catlow he had known for some time as a friend of the family. A dark, rather reserved girl living with an aunt in Leeds, she for her part at first endeavoured to control a passion in him which was characteristically violent. He would have, she told him, to wait. But it was not to be. The climax came during a summer camp at Scarborough of a parish Lads' Club which Geoffrey had accompanied. Miss Catlow was on holiday also, and the two young people soon found each other. There was an evening when they both sang at a Camp Concert of the club. Geoffrey proposed to her. A little later Geoffrey Anketell Studdert Kennedy was married to Emily Catlow, on St. Mark's Day, 1914, in St. Mary's, Quarry Hill, by J. K. Mozley.

The death of Geoffrey's father, followed shortly afterwards by his own departure from Leeds, provided the opportunity for the marriage.

William Studdert Kennedy, Vicar of St. Mary's, Quarry Hill, for thirty-seven years, died in the early months of 1914, aged eighty-eight, in the same place, in the same house, where the large family by his second wife had been brought up. She herself had pre-deceased him by a year. It was the end of the house in Leeds as far as the Studdert Kennedys were concerned. And for Geoffrey himself it was the end of a phase in his life. The whole point of his returning to the place had gone with the death of his father. Considerable efforts, culminating in a deputation of St. Mary's people to the Vicar of Leeds, were made to keep him there. It was felt that he should succeed his father. But authority decided otherwise, as it always wisely does in such matters, and the curate was offered employment in the neighbourhood. But that also was not to be, since Bickersteth at this same time received a letter from a friend who was Archdeacon of Worcester containing the suggestion that, as the living of the small down-town church of St. Paul's, Worcester, was vacant, the man who had already made a name for himself in the diocese during his curacy at Rugby, should go there. Other offers came at the same time. But the reason why Geoffrey chose Worcester was typical. He said to his wife, "St. Paul's has the smallest income and the poorest people —go and look at the house, and if you think you can manage it I will accept."

CHAPTER II

THE VICARAGE IN WORCESTER

HE was instituted to the living on the unpropitious date of June 9th, 1914. St. Paul's, Worcester, belonged, just as St. Mary's, Quarry Hill, had done, to the category of a minor town parish—a church of the little streets put there after the streets had appeared.

Such a setting suited Geoffrey admirably. He valued

the ritual he found there. It was drama: it was beauty, and that always meant enormously much to him. But such things were secondary.

It was all summed in his saying, as once he did, that he would rather, as a matter of personal choice, celebrate the Holy Communion on an upturned packing-case, than amidst the most elaborate ceremonial. Even so, he respected and used ceremonial when it was there.

It was there at St. Paul's, and he used it effectively, in his modest corner of Worcester, as great parish priests of a like kind in an earlier day had done. A colleague of his at Worcester compared him, in fact, to some of the notable clergy of the catholic revival of the previous century.

"He was in the true line of succession of Stanton and Dolling and Wainwright", Hunt, his curate, wrote, "diligent, self-giving, and utterly faithful to the Church system and worship. He loved the daily services and made the most of all the Church offices. He made the baptismal service real for parents and sponsors, and often quoted his poetry to them. His poem 'Christopher' was used on such an occasion . . ."[1]

This is the first appearance of the famous 'poetry', of which in the course of his life Geoffrey wrote a good deal as the emotion of the moment gave cause. It was always the basis of his reputation. Indeed, within three years of these days at St. Paul's, Worcester, his *Rough Rhymes* were selling in edition after edition. For that matter, the appeal of his verse has been maintained and shows no sign of fading. A fourteenth edition of his collected verse appeared in 1947. And three of his poems have even achieved the special distinction of becoming hymns, if rarely sung ones. *Awake, awake to Love and work, Close by the heed-*

[1] *G. A. Studdert Kennedy: By His Friends.*

less worker's side, and *When through the whirl of wheels, and engines humming*.

What would be worth knowing is the effect upon some baptismal party in those far-off days of having read to them by the author the following:

> Bear thou the Christ,
> My little son,
> He will not burden thee,
> That Holy One,
> For, by a mystery,
> Who bearest him he bears,
> Eternally,
> Up to the radiant heights,
> Where Angels be . . .

Perhaps it is as good an indication as any of the odd power of this man that he would make such an action not only acceptable but memorable.

This personal magnetism—and there seems no alternative to the well-known phrase to describe it—was very noticeable, and during the years to come was to be experienced by many people indeed. It had already made itself felt at Rugby, when the masters of the school had heard him as gladly, and been drawn to him as strangely, as the outcasts in the lodging-houses. And now here at Worcester the same process began again. In his first letter in the inevitable parish magazine he had written the trite words: "my study is a place where anyone can come and talk and be sure of a hearty welcome . . . I do want to be a friend to everyone . . ." Ninety-nine out of a hundred earnest young clergymen might have expressed such sentiments without either expecting or receiving any particular response. But this one was different. Within a short time the wife of the new Vicar of St. Paul's had to restrict the numbers of those who wanted what lay behind the 'hearty welcome' and the 'talk'. What they wanted, of course, was to unburden themselves of some of that heavy weight of sins and doubts and secret things which some of the most outwardly normal carry invisibly with them throughout life. So burdened men and women, like mediaeval cripples hobbling to a new shrine, will always tend to respond to such apparently quite inexplicable magnetism as Geoffrey's by seeking him out eagerly, if sometimes furtively, as Nicodemus did Christ by night, and then unloading upon him some of the weight which afflicts them. And always, naturally, there will be among them the cranks, the neurotics, the frauds. The possessor of such magnetism, of which popularity is the counterfeit, or bastard form, is surely much to be pitied, since it is often enough to bear one's own sorrows without having added the infinite weight of so many others. When, years later, Geoffrey told an ordinand who questioned him on the matter that a priest was "one who bore upon himself the sins and sorrows of his people" he certainly knew by that time, from experience, what he was talking about.

This same uncanny power of drawing people was to be seen in operation, when he had been at Worcester only a little while, after the Sunday evening service at St. Paul's. The sedate order of evensong, which flows quietly like a stream in the flat English midlands, which becomes dear only as it becomes familiar, and can be markedly uninspiring to the newcomer, does not generally seem designed to be a high, dramatic occasion. Indeed, it was never intended as such, being rather a choir office for the close of day which the invention of gas lighting, for the first time brought into the evening hours. Herein lay the origin of the social *cachet* for long attached to mattins. The better sort, having leisure to do so, tended to keep their particular rendezvous with Almighty God in the morning. Evensong was for the servants, in such areas where they were to be found, and for the servantless, who by that time might be assumed to have the chores of the day behind them. So it was the humbler sort, domestics and tired mums and dads, who came at evening when the sun was set to the familiar words, "Lighten our darkness we beseech Thee, O Lord . . .", and listen with respect to the sermon. So broad a generalisation obviously cannot be wholly accurate; but it does represent a pattern of social behaviour which was strong when Geoffrey went to St. Paul's in Worcester.

There, evensong soon ceased to be a service and became an experience. "The service," Hunt wrote, "was alive with passion and earnestness. He preached (generally without text or introduction) plunging into his subject at once, and all eyes were riveted on him. He turned the lights out so that people should not be disturbed by the dress or manners of others about them. The effect of this preaching was terrific." After the service came the supplicants, awaiting him in numbers, often each requiring a long and troubled interview: people burdened in conscience, in sexual and domestic difficulty; alcoholics, drug-addicts, and the lonely and the desperate. Such a phenomenon had not been seen in Worcester before, and it is some revelation of the underside of life, even in a Cathedral town in 1914, that it could be seen at all. Yet Geoffrey at St. Paul's somehow seemed to have the power of drawing private anxieties from their various sorrowful obscurities. But it was a costly business: the price to be paid in personal strain was enormous, and continued to bear upon him more or less unremittingly from this time until his death fifteen years later. Once a physician identifies himself with the sufferings of his patients, he is treading a dangerous path. Even the confessional is said to require a certain clinical detachment, and the psychiatrist needs to be the observer and by no means the sharer, of the troubles of those who seek him out. All such relationships between suffering and its treatment are a world away, and exist upon a different plane altogether, from what happens when suffering chances to meet, not treatment, but a love which appears, for some mysterious reason, to need to share its burden. That kind of love, that kind of understanding, Geoffrey had. The trouble is that the world's griefs in the end make a cross so heavy that the bearer of it eventually has to fall under the weight of it. He is in fact doomed as soon as he shoulders the thing. So Geoffrey in Worcester, when the sick in soul came to lay their burdens upon him, had already begun his *via dolorosa*, and hard and long was to be the way of it.

Meanwhile, the quixotic generosities which had annoyed his landlady when he was a curate at Rugby continued at Worcester. The difference was that now he had a wife, and there were times when she found her position required considerable forbearance. There was the occasion, for instance, when he carried a whole bed, by stages, starting with one pillow, from the vicarage to an invalid he had found in comfortless surroundings somewhere in the parish. When she came upon the scene he had progressed as far as the bedstead. The mattress, however, presented difficulties for one man to carry, and so she helped him along the street with it herself. Such stories got about, and were no doubt embroidered in the telling. He was said to be a fool with his money, and therefore soon parted from it. Yet that was not quite true. If indeed he was imprudent with his own, being much addicted to impulsive giving, he was careful enough with that of other people, and very wise in the distribution of the sums which soon began to come to him, often anonymously, to be used as he would.

There was need of it. He had known the place was poor, and gone there largely for that reason. Yet, even so, the extent and bitterness of the poverty he actually encountered there moved him much, and sowed the seeds of his radical political opinions of later years. He was not alone in that; many others, whom circumstances or conscience made aware of the conditions in which a large proportion of the population were living in the early nineteen hundreds, found dangerous thoughts growing within them. Thus Seebohm Rountree. "That in this land of abounding wealth, during a time of perhaps unexampled prosperity, probably more than one fourth of the population is living in poverty is a fact which may well cause great searchings of heart . . . The suffering may be all but voiceless, and we may long remain ignorant of its extent and severity, but when once we realise it we see that social questions of profound importance await solution."[1]

It was true, and unless this search for a solution of economic and social ills, together with the grey poverty which motivated it, be always borne in mind, it is not likely that much of the flavour, at once bitter and anxious, of the whole period through which Geoffrey lived, can be recaptured. The background to it all was the coexistence of poverty and riches.

"It seems strange today," wrote one observer of this scene many years later, "but that some children were hungry was accepted as wet weather is accepted. I can remember my mother helping to serve soup, which could be bought by the needy for a penny a jug. In most towns in the winter such soup was pro-

[1] Seebohm Rountree: *Poverty*. 1901.

37

vided for the poor . . . Neither the tradesmen who provided the materials for the soup, nor the ladies who helped to serve it, appeared to think it wrong that in a rich country families could be in such want that they would queue with jugs for a pennyworth of soup . . . Poverty was something that happened, just as some people were born cripples. You helped; but you did not expect to cure them."[1]

The Socialism of the twenties, the General Strike, the dole queues, the Industrial Christian Fellowship, its crusades and its missions: William Temple and C.O.P.E.C., the whole business of the economic and political thinking of the Church with which, in the unguessed-at future Geoffrey was to be so intimately involved, is without meaning if separated from the continuous drab background against which the high drama of it all was acted out.

The need is to grasp the reality. To what desperate need, one wonders, did Geoffrey carry his bedstead down one of the streets of his Worcester parish? It could have been a case like the one quoted by Jack London, where it was revealed at an inquest on a seventy-seven year old woman, that she had occupied her one filthy room for thirty-five years, had no money, and had died of blood poisoning from bedsores. Such may have been an extreme case; but it was easy enough to find it repeated in any town of Britain. Nor was it necessary to be aged or ill in order to be very poor. The average weekly wage of a working-man in 1913 was twenty shillings. One of the many social investigators of the time, looking into the question of how the family managed on it, concluded that the possession of four children was enough to make the task quite impossible. Given four shillings per child per week for food, there would be four for

[1] Noel Streatfeild: *The Day Before Yesterday.*

the parents and nothing at all for rent or heating or clothing or anything else.[1] Such were the depressing conclusions to which those looking into the state of the working class were faced. Yet there was nothing new about the situation: it had existed for many years, and the back streets of every town contained teeming instances of it. It was thus in the parish of St. Paul's, Worcester. When Geoffrey arrived home penniless, as he often did, to demand of his wife more money to give away, it was with many such situations of need that he was concerned.

All this made no small stir in the place. After the daily Celebration he would be out and about in the parish for the rest of the day. He preached in the streets: there were few homes where he was not a visitor. And of course there were clubs, after the fashion of the day. At Geoffrey's instigation the Church Army opened one, the Captain and his wife living in the vicarage, and evening after evening the peculiar looking vicar with the enormous eyes and noticeable ears would be in one part or another of it. The vicar was also much sought-after by children, just as he had been in Rugby. They followed him about, which can be as exhausting in fact as it is charming in theory. Even so, it was a part of his ministry which he took extremely seriously, giving anxious thought to the schools in the parish, as well as the large Sunday School. Now for obvious reasons it cannot often happen that anyone who involves himself with the young can ever know much about the results. Yet occasionally, and usually long afterwards, a little of the truth is revealed, and it was so in the case of Geoffrey.

Thus, during the General Election Campaign of 1959 a certain Liberal Candidate in the City of Birmingham, a prosperous manufacturer, was asked by a reporter

[1] Mrs. Bember Reeves: *Round About a Pound a Week*. 1913.

for the motivation of his political and social activities, and in particular for his championship of the elderly and the poor. He replied that it was largely an emotional matter, traceable back to his boyhood days, when he came under the influence, as a choir-boy at St. Paul's, in his native Worcester, "of that religious spell-binder, the Rev. G. A. Studdert Kennedy, known to a former generation as 'Woodbine Willie'. 'When he died I resolved to dedicate myself to public service. It was not a political; but an emotional impulse.' "[1]

The interesting thing here is that the speaker, only forty-six at the time of his interview, cannot have known anything of Geoffrey until after the first war, and then but briefly and at a very early age, until Geoffrey's departure in 1921. Yet the deep impression was made, and the influence of the man was a thing of power for long afterwards.

It was at this time also that Geoffrey became known as a conductor of retreats, to use the depressing title given to a function which few can satisfactorily discharge. But with small groups of people who had gone apart for a while to think on things and to pray, Geoffrey was superb. This was the Mary side of an otherwise Martha-like personality, cumbered about to the end with too much to do. Yet somehow he always found time for this 'one thing needful': he was a spiritual interpreter of the first order, and few have more effectively put old wine into new bottles. Not many, in any event, in the years just before the first war, were interested: the idea of 'making a retreat', the religious equivalent of 'getting away from it all', had not gained the general currency it was to do in later years.

Geoffrey became in time very well known as an everyman's guide into that quiet country of the soul. Unfortunately, little of what he said on these occa-

[1] *Birmingham Mail.*

40

sions survives. Except for the book *The New Man in Christ*, edited by the Dean of Worcester after Geoffrey's death, there is little left on record of that abundance which once came from him and which so many found so memorable. This is a sorrowful loss, for he became a great teacher when, after these early Worcester days, and an age away from them in experience, he expressed in this intimate part of his ministry insights given to few. Thus there is this, from an address on prayer in *The New Man in Christ*: "When you pray like Jesus it is clear that you are not asking God to do things for you, you are asking God to give you the desire and the power to do things for him. That is a different story, isn't it? Jesus taught that there was no good thing which God does not desire to give us. The difficulty lies in preparing ourselves to receive, to appreciate, and to use rightly the gifts that he is striving to impart. The tragedy arises from the fact that God cannot give us more than we prepare ourselves to receive. There are in each and all of us unknown and immense capacities for good. We are, indeed, if we would only realise it, the sons of God. All the treasures of an infinite universe of goodness, truth and beauty are ours if we will set ourselves with single minds to seek the highest. But we must ask and keep on asking, we must seek and keep on seeking; we must knock and keep on knocking. Only to those who persevere can the glory of the Kingdom be revealed. The difficulty, according to Jesus, does not lie in persuading God to give; but in preparing ourselves to receive. The Kingdom of God; the fairer, finer, cleaner world, is ours as we ourselves develop our longing and desire for it."

There is also this, from a talk on the 23rd Psalm, a passage typical of the way in which he applied himself not to pietistic detail, but to everyday concerns.

"A really clever man or woman finds it fatally easy not only to deceive others, but to deceive themselves, and justify conduct in themselves which is in reality utterly unjustifiable. Conscious hypocrites are rarer than people suppose, for much that the world calls hypocrisy is the honest strife of very imperfect men. But unconscious hypocrisy is much commoner than people suppose, and the very cleverest men and women are often the victims of it. Their mental powers enable them to impose their own mischievous imaginations upon more simple people and upon themselves. It is never the fool who really wrecks and ruins the family or the nation; it is the able man who has never found the true meaning of life and is still trying to build the world about himself as centre; the man whose hunger of the heart is still unsatisfied and who has not found the great love.

The heart is really the master whether you like it or not, and if the master be wrong the servants can but do his will. If the light that is within them be darkness, how great is that darkness!

The supreme question for us all is, what do you want? What do you love? And it is here that the Good Shepherd comes in to minister to our necessity —our necessity, let us repeat—comes in to give us not luxuries and extras, but comes in to give us what we must have. If we pretend that we can do without it, we do but deceive ourselves. If we do not love Beauty, Truth and Goodness as it is in Jesus Christ we will love some beauty, truth and goodness of our own, some person or reality. If we will not have Jesus for our Good then we must either find a better one, or serve a worse. If we pretend that we have not got one we are merely fooling ourselves. Atheism is not a creed, it is a nervous disease; it means life without anything to live for, and that is hell.

When a man tells me that he has no religion I simply take it that he is talking nonsense and proceed to find out what his religion is—what it is that gives life meaning to him. What one generally discovers is that the man or woman has a god, but a poor one. And because he has a poor god he is a poor person and is still in want, not knowing what he wants, but unhappy till he gets it."

But apart from these collected retreat addresses in *The New Man in Christ* only fragments remain, and even these are scattered about in unexpected places. A little book, for instance, called *When We Pray, a Method of Prayer taught by Studdert Kennedy*[1] brought out, again after Geoffrey's death, by an admirer, is clearly based on notes taken of some of his talks. Moreover, anyone who cares to compare the 'method' with which the book is concerned with much subsequent popular teaching on this theme will find in fact that there is the original and prototype of a good deal of it. The man who, in the Deanery of Worcester, or in the Chapel at Earl Beauchamp's house at Madresfield, used to conduct retreats for little groups of earnest people was, in fact, potentially a spiritual counsellor of the first order, a great deal of whose value was that he seemed to say:

Everyman, I will go with thee and be thy guide,
In thy most need, to go by thy side.

But then, of course, that event occurred which came in time to render all else insignificant. The world blew up, to the profound astonishment of all concerned, who do not seem to have noticed the fuse burning and sparking in their midst for so long. Three months after Geoffrey had gone to Worcester, the first world war began. How that involved him, falls now to be told.

[1] Ronald Sinclair: *When We Pray*. Hodder & Stoughton.

43

It was a fine summer, that one of 1914. Down among the streets of the parish of St. Paul's in the Blockhouse, Worcester, the heat drew odours from the privies out back of the row of houses facing the vicarage. That itself was a pleasant enough house. Its front door, flush to the street, gave on to a hall from which stairs led to dining-room and study. At the side, an unexpectedly large garden, brick wall enclosed, stretched down to the church. In these surroundings, for the three months remaining between his institution and the outbreak of war, the new vicar devoted himself to getting the feel of his first parish.

Meanwhile, the country at large drifted into that summer, like a man in a punt out for the day who, having had some narrow squeaks with other craft at his setting out, now sensed calmer waters before him. For one thing, industrial relations seemed to have settled down, for a while at least. Strikes and lock-outs, epidemic two years before, had tailed off. Britain prospered; some people were making a lot of money, and for those who were not, the old-age pensions and insurance schemes at long last had smoothed the sharper edges of poverty. Ireland, of course continued to give trouble. Indeed, throughout that spring by far the most alarming news had come from across the Irish Sea. Carson had raised his Ulster Volunteers, as the possibility of Home Rule drew nearer. Civil war had seemed very close. And then, to cap all, had come the mutiny at the Curragh where officers of troops, concentrated for a possible move against the North, had announced that they would send in their papers rather than obey such an order. When the new Vicar of St. Paul's, Worcester, had time to read a paper in those months in his new parish, such were the events making the headlines.

Meanwhile, life went on. The British fleet paid a

courtesy call on the German Naval review at Kronstadt, where the great ships of both countries lay alongside each other, bathed in the sunlight of that unusually flaming June. The occasion, overflowing with mutual goodwill, seemed a pleasant sequel to the State visit of King George V to Paris which had taken place in June.

In fact, by the end of July, things were distinctly improved compared with the situation earlier in the year.

In view of all this it was scarcely surprising that a news item which came at the end of June created at first little stir. "The Archduke Francis Ferdinand, heir to the throne of Austro-Hungary and his morganatic wife, the Duchess of Hohenburg, were assassinated yesterday in the town of Sarajevo, Capital of Bosnia." The best-documented pot-shot in the history of the world soon began to make its consequences felt. They appeared to be endless: they continued to accumulate: they touched the lives of the most obscure, including even that of the new Vicar of St. Paul's, Worcester.

But not immediately. First there had to be the period of those far-off battles among the alien corn in the golden autumn: Mons, the Marne, the Aisne: when French and German faced each other in open field, and the small British Expeditionary Force, landed in France on August 21st, learned to know the long, poplar-lined French roads. These were great, these were earth-shaking events. But because happenings of half a century old are still in that limbo which exists between the historical and the contemporary, the feel of those months, August to December 1914, is difficult to recapture. Waterloo is easier to visualise than Mons, having settled into the stylised postures of history. But the rifle fire of Mons can still faintly be heard down the corridors of living memory.

Yet it is important—at any rate to a narrative such as this—to see again that sequence of events, since only by doing so is it possible even to guess at the emotions which made people living them, including Geoffrey, act subsequently as they did. Something tremendous clearly had happened in the world to make H. G. Wells so far abandon his former attitudes as to write, in a letter to *The Daily News* towards the end of this August: "I find myself enthusiastic for this war against Prussian militarism. We are, I believe, assisting at the end of a vast, intolerable oppression upon civilisation."

Geoffrey, in his small corner, apparently shared these sentiments. His parish magazine for September contained this: "I cannot say too strongly that I believe every able-bodied man ought to volunteer for service anywhere. There ought to be no shirking of that duty. Those who cannot volunteer for military service can pray . . ."

There were many saying such things by then, who were later much mocked for doing so by those sadder and wiser after the event. Geoffrey himself became sadder and wiser after the event. It was long held, indeed, to have been especially monstrous for the Church to have urged Christian soldiers onward as to war with such crude abandon. He came to think so himself. Such sentiments were duly taken down and used in evidence at the trial of the Establishment, in the wider sense of the word, which came years later. Not that it matters now, of course. The whole scene has been long buried deep beneath other deposits of history. But he who cares to excavate down to it cannot avoid finding there, like a golden ornament among much that is worthless, traces of that astonishing wave of brave emotion which then animated so many. And unless he takes cognisance of this, recognising it as the true metal that it was, he will be unable to make head or tail of what happened.

What happened then was that, absolutely for the first time, a genuine dragon was felt to be at large, and St. George called upon to deal with him. Out of what long camouflaged lair he had so suddenly emerged no one seemed quite to know. It was difficult at first even to credit that he had. But as Mons gave place to the Marne, as the casualty lists began to come in, as France began to bleed to death, as Paris escaped by the skin of its teeth, as Antwerp was bombarded and fell and the first Belgian refugees arrived—seventy thousand of them by October—it was seen that this dragon was real enough. He breathed fire, his proportions were enormous, his intentions wholly evil—and he was made in Germany. And then, hard upon the shock of these events came stories of atrocities, all the more horrifying because falling upon ears innocent of the sound of propaganda: tales of rape and pillage; of children skewered on bayonets by derisive Prussians, and girls set aside for the pleasure of monocled officers. Of course, most of the stories were untrue. Such was one of the many disenchanting disclosures of subsequent history. The German general staff, in fact, actually appointed a commission of neutral American observers to investigate these charges. The result was as might have been expected: occupying troops had acted with brutality: but since war was brutal anyway that was not surprising. Even so, the effect of it all in conditioning the response of many a gallant soul was considerable.

It was not difficult in those times to induce belief, however extravagant. In some cases no inducement was necessary. By the autumn of 1914 it was an article of faith that Russian troops had been seen trying to force roubles into slot machines at London termini, and several railwaymen testified to having found snow in the compartments of trains which had been used for their transportation. But there was also another cause of credulity. The war itself, especially the vastness of its scale and the suddenness of its onset, was so improbable that, to some who considered the matter, it became explicable only in cosmic terms as a fore-ordained final conflict between good and evil. In other words, God came into the picture: and if God came into the picture, so did the Church. Had there not been, for instance, as was widely believed, Angels at the Battle of Mons, interposing themselves between the advancing enemy and the thin lines of British? A certain clergyman, by name the Reverend A. A. Boddy, having investigated the matter, had no doubts, and published his conclusions in a pamphlet which had a wide sale. That is not surprising. Mr. Boddy's account of his interview with a wounded private of the Lincolnshire Regiment is interesting.

"They could now see the oncoming flood of Germans in close formation . . . There was a tremendous fire on both sides. The noise was terrific. Suddenly all guns ceased, as by magic. 'What's up?' the men cried. They looked fearlessly over the top of the barricade. This is what they saw—thirty yards away there were four or five BEINGS larger than men. They had their faces towards the oncoming Germans, and each one had its arms stretched out horizontally from its shoulders, and was slowly moving them up and down, with a sort of suggestion of 'Stop and go back. You must not come any farther'."[1]

Such testimony, and such support, were alike valuable to military authority faced with the task of raising a volunteer army. So Mr. Boddy's pamphlet appeared, "With permission of the Official Censor."

[1] A. A. Boddy: *Real Angels of Mons.*

What Geoffrey wrote in his parish magazine for September 1914 was being re-echoed in similar quarters all over the country. The results of such appeals, and of many other far larger ones, were impressive. The Bishop of London, Winnington Ingram, after a recruiting speech in which he described the war "as the greatest fight ever made for the Christian religion", was thanked by the War Office for adding 10,000 men to the forces of the Crown. "The acknowledgement could equally well have gone to Horatio Bottomley", a critic justly observed many years later, "and he was prosecuted for fraud".[1] By the middle of the month the daily intake of recruits was thirty thousand: and there were difficulties over billeting them. True, not everyone was for war. An intellectual minority was violently against it, and was allowed to express itself with surprising freedom. Thus A. G. Gardiner in *The Daily News* in October: "The soldier who has the luck to come out of the war alive will emerge as poor as he went in; but the shareholders of Krupps and Armstrongs will have the wealth of the Indies as their reward."

It may have been true. On the other hand, the threat behind the events, fast becoming increasingly global, which the papers daily so alarmingly reported, was a very real one. The virgins of Worcester, or of any other English city, might not in fact have been imperilled if German battalions had marched in there as they had already done into Ghent, and Rheims and Antwerp. But England would: and it was after all something to slip out from work one day to the nearest recruiting office, there to take oath before a pince-nezed officer and a big-bellied Boer War sergeant, to defend King and Country, in the honest belief, by

[1] Anthony Howard : *The Baldwin Age*. Ed. John Raymond. Eyre & Spottiswoode.

no means necessarily false, that one was thereby assisting, however humbly, St. George to slay the dragon. This honest belief, this generous emotion, this absolute conviction that the contest was starkly between Right and Wrong was that alone which made the volunteer principle work in an unprecedented situation. Soon there were many blank chairs in offices, key men gone from factories, an emptiness along one side of many a matrimonial bed.

"Most of these volunteers of the prime," wrote C. E. Montague, "were men of handsome and boundless illusions. Each of them quite seriously thought of himself as a molecule in the body of a nation that was really, and not just figuratively, straining every nerve to discharge an obligation of honour."[1]

So, as the leaves fluttered down that autumn, as, on the eastern front, a hundred thousand Russian dead sank into the ooze of the Pripet Marshes after Tannenburg, as one hundred and twenty thousand German dead mingled their bones with the wreckage of the old British regular army after the first battle of Ypres, as the opposing armies dug themselves in from the Channel to the Alps, the first and the last great volunteer army ever raised in Britain began to mass. A memorable poster became ubiquitous: the face of Kitchener, staring eyes over handlebar moustache and pointing finger. Many of those who responded found themselves at first frustrated. Many were called: few seemed to be chosen, especially for commissions. If, as Geoffrey urged in his magazine, every able-bodied man ought to volunteer for service, it often proved quite difficult to get taken on, so that various voluntary organisations came into existence to expedite the process. However, by the early months of 1915 the machinery was beginning to work more

[1] C. E. Montague: *Disenchantment.*

smoothly: tens of thousands of men, in uniform for the first time in their lives, began military training. One of the centres chosen was Worcester.

The Dean of Worcester, W. Moore Ede, invited Geoffrey to preach in the Cathedral to the two thousand or so men who were paraded there on three Sunday mornings of 1915. It was the fruitful decision of one who was already a friend and admirer. To the end of Geoffrey's life, indeed, this friendship of Moore Ede's was constant. And now both friendship and admiration were strengthened by the younger man's achievement in making, out of the highly unpromising situation of a church parade—something which was not uncommonly regarded as one of the rigours of war—an experience which many of the men remembered for as long afterwards as was granted to them.

They were not an easy audience. No congregation gathered together under duress ever is. What is more, they were men living through a rare intensity of experience. "Who," asked C. E. Montague, in a passage which enshrines forever the mood of such men in that distant time, "of all those who were in camp and still are alive, will not remember until he dies the second boyhood that he had in the late frosts and then in the spring and early summer of 1915? The awakening bird-notes of Reveillé at dawn, the two-mile run through auroral mists breaking over a still inviolate England . . . the peace of the tranquil hours on guard at some sequestered post, alone with the sylvester moonlight . . . and the jocund days of marching and digging trenches in the sun . . ."[1]

Such men could be as critical as they were lively. Discipline, sometimes deeply resented, duly set them down in the Cathedral after an infinity of bawlings

[1] ibid.

without, and the certainty of more to follow at the marching away. To hold such a gathering, and to hold them fast, required powers in a preacher of an unusual order. Geoffrey seemed to have them. Here was an opportunity, superb as unexpected, to use for good the greatest of his many gifts—oratory. There was not a cough, not a shuffling of feet, when he was speaking. It was all familiar, homely stuff, starting invariably from the known and going on to the unknown, so that a talk about a conversation overheard in a barber's shop on the need to treat the enemy worse than they were alleged to have treated the Belgians, passed easily and enthrallingly to the whole matter of the conquest of evil by good. It sounds banal: but behind it was the compelling, odd personality of the man himself. Quite soon, Geoffrey's Sunday sermon was a talking point in the camps for the following week.

Meanwhile, there was a personal problem much exercising him: the question of when and how he should get into the army himself. It was a considerable dilemma. In France the matter was settled for the priest, who was liable to be drafted with the rest, and there was a body of opinion in England which held that the same rule should apply there also. The situation was by no means clear. As a matter of fact, as Archbishop Davidson lamented in 1914, it was "chaotically unsolved", and remained so until the end. So in some clerical hearts, at any rate, there was ardent desire to serve as best they could. That meant a chaplaincy to the forces, something by no means easy to attain. For one thing, any man in charge of a parish had first himself to make provision for his duties to be carried out in his absence. For another, he had to persuade his bishop to release him. And yet again he had to commend himself to military authority in the form of the Royal Army Chaplain's Department. That meant a visit to the War Office and an interview with a remarkable character, Bishop Taylor Smith, Chaplain General. He was not regarded with unmixed approval. Already, in the closing months of 1914, his pronounced evangelical predispositions had brought down upon him the anger of the English Church Union and Lord Halifax, who considered the Chaplain General deficient in sympathy towards Anglo-Catholic applicants for chaplaincies. They even memorialised Lord Kitchener on the matter, though without decisive result. Perhaps there were other things on his mind at the time. One thing, however, which Bishop Taylor Smith did understand was death. At least he had a great interest in the subject, and his insistence upon the need, by the chaplain, for adequate preparation of the wounded for that event was long remembered. The impression was left that death would have taken place, and possibly rigor mortis set in, before the Bishop's injunctions could be carried out with the thoroughness he enjoined.

But once these various hurdles were cleared the rest of the course was often surprisingly, even alarmingly rapid. Within days a man could find himself in a position to visit a military tailor and emerge to astonish himself by his own reflection in a mirror, with only his collar and the Maltese cross of the department upon his badges to indicate the nature of his office, and his own inner resources to make of it either a mockery or a splendour.

CHAPTER III

THE MAKING OF WOODBINE WILLIE

ALL these things happened to Geoffrey: the initial difficulties and delays followed by the extremely rapid conclusion to the matter. On December 21st, 1915, he was appointed Temporary Chaplain to the Forces. On Christmas Day he found himself in a French village contemplating four hundred troops drawn up in sluicing rain waiting, no doubt with mixed feelings, for a service. Soon afterwards, in a letter to the people of St. Paul's, reprinted in the local paper—the first of many such—he described the scene.

"It was pouring rain, and the roads were very heavy. Everywhere along the road one met troops, mud up to their knees, dripping wet, but always with a greeting ready, or a joke. The first place we were due was a little French village which in summer and in happier times must be a beautiful place; but it was desolate that Christmas morning, the road a quagmire, cut into ruts and hollows by the heavy traffic, and the hedges covered with mud. I found about four hundred men drawn up in the rain waiting . . .

"I hurried into my robes and went to the middle of the square. There was of course no instrument, and I thanked God for a voice like a fog-horn. But once we started on 'Come all ye faithful' no instrument and no leading voice were necessary. They sang with all their might . . . Then the glorious part came—I went to a shed in the farmyard, and the communicants came to me. There were not many; but they meant it. No lights, no ritual, nothing to help but the rain and the far-off roll of guns, and Christ was born in a cattle-shed on Christmas Day."

Thus began the wartime ministry of a man destined to become, through personal qualities and the accident of circumstances, the most celebrated army padre of all time: and one who was to end hating with a rare bitterness the whole enterprise to which, at this beginning, he went with such naïvety. The same thing happened to many others; but most of them died in their anger. He survived, and told the tale.

Soon, anyway, he was to be introduced to far less idyllic scenes than Holy Communion in a cattle shed on Christmas Day. His account continues:

"On the Monday I received orders to leave for the great base of the British Army. For a while I have said good-bye to the happy part of army work, and have come to the sad part of it. I am not in a hospital; I am chaplain to the troops quartered in the town, and it is sad because here is the old enemy one fights—sin—and sin is sadder than sorrow. Had I a boy I would pray that he might never be long at a base—."

The place was Rouen, and it was quite appalling. To recapture the reality behind the parsonic language it is necessary only to rummage among the extensive, sombre literature of that most sombre of all wars. "Passing through the town," one private soldier wrote years afterwards, "we saw stretching from the Red Lamp and down the street about three hundred men in a queue, all waiting their turns, the majority being mere lads. 'I expect they're determined to have a short time before they go West tomorrow', Duffy said."[1]

That particular brothel, as it happened, was not in Rouen; but plenty could be found there like it. As the war became static, and the bases grew until they were vast cities of men, the evil inseparable from such immense concentrations grew in proportion. They were well under way in Rouen by the time Geoffrey arrived there in the January of 1916. In that town low-lying on the banks of the Seine, the starting point for drafts going up to the unknown terrors of the line, many a newcomer, heartsick, lonely, totally unequipped for the experience, could find himself, with simple astonishment, looking in his leisure moments into the mouth of an alcoholic and bawdy hell patrolled by military police.

[1] Frank Richards: *Old Soldiers Never Die.*

It is against such a background that the quality of Geoffrey's achievement during the four months he was at Rouen needs to be measured. He was as raw a newcomer as any. Fortunately, there was at Rouen, in the person of D. F. Carey, as assistant Chaplain General, a man of wisdom and understanding. When Geoffrey reported to him with the request to be given work in a hospital, Carey told him briefly there were no vacancies. There was, however, a canteen down by the *Rive Gauche* Siding run by Lady Mabel Egerton, where reinforcements coming from Le Havre on their way up to the line spent the last few hours before entraining. Geoffrey could go there. It seemed to Carey that was the very place for a man who, in the same interview, when asked about his background, said he had once been a revolutionary agnostic socialist, whatever that may mean, who used to stand on a tub and talk in public places in the Midlands. So to the canteen by the *Rive Gauche* Siding he went.

To ask what exactly he was supposed to do, faced with the smoky tumult of such a place, is to pose the problem of the padre in an extreme form. It is a problem which reaches a good deal further than this particular manifestation of it. What, indeed, is the place of the parson in the scheme of things when some extraordinary circumstance pulls him out of the sometimes distressingly little world in which he lives and moves and has his being? Unlike the doctor, or any other technologist, he does not seem to have any self-evident place, a fact which can only too easily lead to the conclusion that he does not deserve one. Furthermore, if he is to become necessary, he has first to create the need. The alternative is to shelter behind such protection as rank and privilege afford, an alternative more easily acceptable in proportion as the man concerned is not of a thoughtful or a sensitive kind. It is a problem which can rarely have presented itself quite so acutely as to the army chaplains of the war to which Geoffrey went.

They were the first of their kind ever to be involved in a situation of total war, and they went untrained and unprepared from the parochial round, the common task. And though the parochial round might, in happier times, have furnished all they needed to ask, it was far otherwise when they found themselves in places like the *Rive Gauche* Siding at Rouen. Not surprisingly, some failed. The Army Chaplain of 1914–18 certainly had a bad press after the war, though any attempt to assess its accuracy must allow for the fact that in any age part of the function of the Church and its representatives is to act as whipping boys for the dissatisfied.

"If ever the conversation veered round to native troops or parsons," Private Frank Richards wrote in *Old Soldiers Never Die*, recalling post-war talks with an ex-member of his battalion, "he would launch out with a flow of language which on two occasions was very nearly the cause of us being turned out of the pubs we were in. By stop-tap he generally had thousands of native troops in one spittoon and thousands of parsons in the other." When Geoffrey came to die, hundreds of men not unlike Frank Richards and his drinking companion spoke of him with characteristic sentimentality as "our fallen comrade", and in Liverpool placed a packet of Woodbines on his coffin. But the bad press was a fact.

Chiefly, the charge preferred against the chaplain seems to have been one of inadequacy. Some of the criticisms are more touching than was perhaps intended. Siegfried Sassoon, in *Memoirs of an Infantry Officer*, in a few lines painted a picture which haunts

57

the mind. The scene was a casualty clearing station; with many wounded, covered in the blood and filth of their condition. One person on that horrific stage who seemed to have no part to play was a chaplain, "discovering the inadequacies of the ministry of the Church of England." Was he? One wonders. Across the years, something of the plight of that unhappy man comes through the print. And with it comes also a great and looming question—the one which Geoffrey spent the rest of his days struggling with—what is the meaning of suffering? The Church of England is not alone in finding the answer to that one difficult.

But perhaps the most memorable of all the adverse criticisms which fell upon the chaplains was C. E. Montague's celebrated chapter *The Sheep that Were Not Fed*, in *Disenchantment*. There were all sorts and conditions of men among them, he states, some good, some bad; like the chaplain "drunk at dinner in Gobert's restaurant in Amiens on the evening of one of the bloodiest days of the first battle of the Somme." But mostly the quality was indifferent. "There was the man who, urged by national comradeship, would have been a soldier but that his bishop banned it: to be an army chaplain was the next best thing. There was the man who, urged by a different instinct, felt irresistibly that at the moment the war was the central thing in the whole world and that it was unbearable not to be at the centre of things. And there was, in great force, the large, healthy, pleasant young curate . . . He abounded so much that whenever now one hears the words 'Army Chaplain' his image springs up of itself in the mind."[1]

The inadequacy of such was all the more sadly evident, Montague held, in view of the rare oppor-

[1] C. E. Montague: *Disenchantment*.

tunity with which they were presented. Living with death a constant probability, torn out of the complacencies of life at home, yet with long hours in trench or billet in which to think about things, some men were rendered unusually receptive to spiritual things. It is a surprising judgment. War is generally as bad for religion as for anything else. However, there was Montague's verdict: the opportunity was presented: the average chaplain was unable to grasp it. True, he was usually genial, he tended to be overpoweringly man to man; he gave away cigarettes in large quantities. But that was not enough. "When you are given an infant earth to fashion out of a whirling ball of flaming metals and gases, then good humour, some taste for adventure, a jolly way with the men . . . may not carry you far. You may come off, by no fault of your own, like the curate in Shakespeare who was put up to play Alexander the Great: 'A marvellous good neighbour, i' faith, and a very good bowler: but, for Alexander—alas, you see how 'tis—a little o'er-parted.' "[1]

Yet who was adequate to the monstrous challenge of such a time? Most men, when weighed in that balance, were found wanting. It is difficult to wander much through the vast, sad, yet endlessly fascinating museum of that old war without being impressed by the extraordinary brainlessness with which it seems to have been conducted on the higher levels. There seems often remarkably little of original thought inside the mind of a Haig or a Joffre: only a few predetermined attitudes, chiefly connected with notions of patriotism and duty, and in some a streak of personal ambition—as in the case of the disastrous French General Nivelle—all the more astonishing because cultivated at the price of massive human sac-

[1] ibid.

rifice. Who indeed was adequate? "It is only a very limited number of men," Archbishop Davidson sensibly observed, "of any sort of class or profession, who would be fit at such a juncture to do all that was needed." Not the generals, not the statesmen, certainly. It can scarcely be surprising if the divines were not, either. One emerges from that ghastly museum of the old war with a shudder, wondering whether we are any better off now, even after another war has been and gone or whether, even among our nuclear war-heads, the higher direction of human affairs is not still waiting for the cavalry to break through.

"Imagine the religious revival," Montague goes on to say, "if some man of apostolic genius had had the fishing of the troubled waters."[1]

It was quite untrue, of course. Religious revivals are not brought about by men, even of apostolic genius; but by the Spirit of God moving upon the face of the waters. All that such men can do—and there was one of them in early 1915 making a clown of himself for Christ's sake in the *Rive Gauche* Siding at Rouen—is to touch a few lives with a great love, to open a few eyes to a splendid vision, and often to break his own heart in the process.

There were also other elements present in the situation of a chaplain which could be disturbing. Pressure of circumstances in that war could easily transform him into a combination of entertainments manager, welfare officer, and undertaker, and often did. He could be, all too easily, made to appear and feel useless, like a man wandering round a burning ship exchanging pleasantries with the fire parties. And because of his association with formal occasions like church parade he could be associated all too

[2] ibid.

easily—and indeed often justly—with the more repellent aspects of the military system. When to these considerations is added the fact that his was in some measure a privileged position, and that he could, in the first war, go home when his term of service was up, the background of his difficulties becomes even more forbidding.

Such handicaps were in some cases so triumphantly overcome by exceptional men that the first war produced padres whose names became public property, notwithstanding the severe criticism to which their kind in general was later subjected. Of these, Geoffrey's fame was by far the most widespread. But there were others, like Tubby Clayton, founder of Toc H, who were able in some measure to sublimate the horrors of it all and elevate the concepts of sacrifice and service. And there were others yet again, like the saintly T. B. Hardy, v.c., m.c., d.s.o., whom we shall meet in due course, whom no breath of criticism could reach.

Even so, there was, as indeed there must always be, one inner difficulty in the chaplain's position in time of war of which it is surprising to find so little awareness in a man as sensitive as Geoffrey—the question as to whether he had any business to be an official part of a system dedicated to the prosecution of a war which, the longer it continued, was increasingly seen as a crime against humanity. It is true that he came to see it as such himself.

> Waste of Blood, and waste of Tears
> Waste of youth's most precious years,
> Waste of ways the Saints have trod
> Waste of Glory, Waste of God—
> War!

Such emotional denunciations became, and have remained, common enough. They formed the basis of the pacifism of the twenties and thirties. But here and there it was a fact that, during the first war, the chaplain could find himself in a difficult position. Such an one was the unfortunate man in one of P. B. Clayton's *Plain Tales from Flanders, The Story of M—*, wherein it is related that a devout Major of Signals became so appalled by the bloody consequences of his own handiwork that he went down to G.H.Q., entered unannounced, and informed his G.O.C. of his intention of ceasing to carry out his duties as from noon that day. The General sent for the Corps Chaplain who "tried, poor fellow, to do his best by proving once again the justice of our Cause. M— told me, in a lucid moment later, that this was the most appalling agony of it all, and that he had the greatest difficulty in not treating him as Paul once treated the High Priest."[1]

M— was lucky. They said he was mad, and put him in an asylum. If he had been a ranker he might have been put against a wall, in which case no doubt some other padre would have been called upon to offer the consolations of religion. Fortunately, such extreme challenges did not come the way of many. But the possibility of them was always there, and it seems strange that there is so little reflection of their inner strain upon the Christian conscience in the writings of Geoffrey coming out of the war years. On the contrary, he seems at times to have allowed himself gladly to be used as a morale-booster to an extent which would certainly have been regarded as improper in a chaplain of the second war. Of the challenge to the whole Christian position which the war brought with it he was, God knows, profoundly concerned. His response to the challenge forms the basis of his teaching. But he does not seem to have

[1] P. B. Clayton: *Plain Tales from Flanders.*

been aware of the challenge implicit therein to the whole position of a priest in uniform. It seems a curious blind spot; but who is to judge after all these years, or presume to say what he thinks should have been done in so fearful a situation, especially anyone who was not there on that St. Crispin's Day, or any other, for that matter? Without a doubt, the tensions of Geoffrey's work pressed terribly upon him as the years passed, and inner doubts of this sort may well have been among them. But at the beginnings there is no sign of it. The war was a just Cause. He was in that stage at Rouen in the early months of 1916. And now we can get back to him and find what happened there.

A yellow cutting from a local paper, quoting a letter of Geoffrey's of that time, has at any rate his version. To those who would seek after the atmosphere of those 'old, unhappy, far-off things', it has its own fascination.

"My chief work during the day lies at the station. Men on their way to the front are often confined there from 3 a.m. to 5.30 p.m. I go down about two o'clock and go into the coffee-shop to find it filled with men. There is a piano in the corner with generally a crowd round it. I go to the piano and begin to sing, one song after another until I'm tired, then I get up and tell the men I'm there to help them in any way I can. I have found it comforts wives and mothers to hear from me that I have seen their loved soldiers and talked to them, so I always offer to send for anyone who wants it a letter I have printed saying I have seen them. Before the men come with their addresses, which they do in crowds, we have some prayers for those at home. After the service the procession begins . . . some will show me their photographs, the bright girl face in the clean white blouse . . ."

Generally, before the interviews were ended, a sergeant was heard yelling out the fall-in. It was generally growing dark by then, and in the gloom a huge long train was standing.

It was then Geoffrey's custom to go down the train distributing cigarettes out of one haversack and New Testaments out of the other. To the end he was still giving away Woodbines.

"I begin at the top of the train; and work down it, going into each carriage. I look round into their faces. I can always tell the man who has taken that trip before. You can see it in his eyes . . . So on for an hour (it always stands an hour), with the knapsacks growing lighter and a lump in the throat that grows bigger. Often I have to cling on to finish the last carriages, creeping along the footboard. At last, I am left alone looking after the disappearing tail-lights. There is nothing glorious about this departure. It is all sordid and filthy. God only knows the hardships men endure on these journeys in packed and dirty carriages. No place to wash, no place to move, they sit and wait for eighteen hours or more until, I suppose, they hear far off the sound of guns and know that the end is near . . ."

He was soon himself to hear the sound of those guns and to have any suppositions removed as to what happened at the end of the line.

Meanwhile, he would wander back to the canteen when the rumble of the train had faded, to drift into that now empty place for a meal. He rarely seemed to know what he was eating. Often it was some left-overs he picked up from the plates still littering the room. And frequently, when the women running the place cooked him a meal and substituted the scraps for something better, it was observed that he did not notice the changeover.

In Rouen, in the Lent of 1916, there took place a remarkable series of meetings in the Hotel de Ville and in the camps around the town, in which Geoffrey was the chief figure. Carey had already discovered the newcomer's exceptional powers, and now had resolved to give them scope. And though it is no doubt unlikely that many of those who came to the meetings —most of them destined for the great carve-up on the Somme in a few months time—were particularly concerned with the sacred season, yet their response to the challenge Geoffrey tried to put before them was genuine enough. More than that, it was staggering. The foundations of his fame were laid down at this point, thereafter to be built upon by report and rumour. Yet, examined long afterwards, what he said— published later as *Rough Talks of a Padre*—seems trite enough. Spoken against the background of the soul-rotting evils of the base, it was a challenge to self-dedication, a period piece with its characteristic first-war idealisation of the soldier dead and "the cause for which they died." Something of the progress of this astonishing effort he described in a letter home.

"We started with a hall fairly full. The number grew until we were crammed, with men standing on the gangway and sitting on the edge of the platform. The whole object of the lectures was to put the challenge of Christ before the men and make them hear. It is wonderful, the change that war had already worked in the souls of many. I can see them now; crammed, packed and seething, sitting on the platform round my feet, a mass of brown, eager faces. The climax came on Good Friday when the hall was packed. When it was over, they sat still for a while, and I am sure Christ was with us, and was glad. Then they cheered, and their cheer was an answer to the call of Christ. Some may forget it; but surely not all; some will remember that Good Friday night for years."

Perhaps some did, some who survived. But that innocence of spirit which the whole incident enshrines was soon to die, with so much else. The same packet of letters and cuttings which contained this letter of Geoffrey's held also, on another yellowed piece of paper, a piece of verse, written only a year later, which evokes a very different scene:

> There's a Jerry over there, Sarge!
> Can't you see 'is big square 'ead?
> If 'e moves again I'll get 'im,
> Take these glasses 'ere and see.
> What's that? Got 'im through the 'ead, Sarge?
> Where's my blarsted cup o' tea!

Into such scenes Geoffrey passed when, in the June of 1916, in time for the Somme offensive, he was posted to that now-forgotten thing, the Front, as padre with the 157th Brigade of the 46th Division. It was the first of three periods of battle experience. The second was in the following year, with the 17th Brigade of the 24th Division, when he was in the attack on the Messines Ridge, preceded by the horrific dawn blowing of the mines which lifted the top from that geographical feature, and buried a great many Germans in an explosion heard across the Channel in Kent. In the last year of the war, with the 42nd Division, he was in the final advance. It was quite a lot. That it was not more was due, not to his own wish, but to the direction of the Deputy Chaplain General, Bishop Gwynne, sometime of the Sudan, a great man of much wisdom whose appointment as Bishop in charge of all chaplains in France had been Archbishop

Davidson's quiet solution of the difficulties arising from the alleged partialities of Taylor Smith. Clearly, Gwynne recognised in Geoffrey a very rare bird, and used him accordingly. The consequence was that, between his periods in the line, he was given a series of special postings. One would seem in the retrospect to have been a task of considerable difficulty—to wander through the whole army area speaking on behalf of one of the most curious enterprises ever undertaken by a Church in the middle of a war, the National Mission of Repentance and Hope. Another was to act as chaplain, at various times, to three Army Infantry Schools. A third, the most extraordinary of all, saw him attached to a School for Physical and Bayonet Training, sometimes going on tour with a gruesome collection of morale-boosters which included a champion boxer, two wrestlers, and an N.C.O. whose title to fame was that he had killed eighteen Germans with a bayonet. One of the high spots of this performance was that Geoffrey would asthmatically box with the boxer, for the edification of troops.

What on earth does it all add up to? How could it be that, out of this mad medley of clowning and genius, of sentimentality and profound thought upon the sins and sufferings of man, out of an outward gaiety and an inwardly breaking heart, there should have emerged one of the most famous figures of that old war? Even that question would not, at this distance of time, be worth the answering were it not for another and a greater one lying behind. How did it come that this man was able to make God real to so many to whom he seemed to be dead? How was it that, over and over again, the most unlikely people came, not only to love and remember him, but through him to get a glimpse of a splendour far beyond the customary horizons of ordinary life?

Somewhere in the answer lies the secret at the heart of religion; but it is a secret he took with him, and nobody seems since to have possessed it. Certainly, the common people heard him gladly. But why? As well ask, perhaps, why the common people once streamed out on to the hillsides of Galilee. The answer is but partially to be found in the written records in either case. There must have been something highly unusual, in more ways than one, about the man himself. Odd stories of Geoffrey which have stuck in the memories of now ageing people testify to that.

Thus a lady, now elderly, remembers how, as a young V.A.D. nurse given to taking solitary Sunday walks in the dunes around Hardelot, south of Boulogne, she used to be puzzled by the crowds of men around a hut which lay at a distance. They filled the hut: they clustered upon the dunes. And always some would climb on to the roof and hold themselves in such a position that they could see and hear through the occasional window. The place was used for voluntary church services by men on a course at the School of so-called Physical and Bayonet Training (actually an establishment for the re-habilitation of the disaffected at a time when considerable numbers were becoming so). Who could be the padre? Investigation revealed him as the ugliest man she had ever seen, with a pair of wonderful brown eyes and the terrible cough, familiar to nurses by that time, of the gassed. That was the sound that would wake her, back in Hardelot, on some week-day mornings. She would get up, peep out of her convalescent home window down on to the grey-dawn street and the solid-tyred transport gathered there. And there he would be; looking pretty desolate, going back up the line with a returning draft. The next Sunday there would be scarcely a soul at the hut out among the dunes.

Sometimes, she discovered, he only just arrived there himself. He loved riding: the Commandant of the School gave him a horse; the horse ran away with him one Sunday morning, round and round the local golf-course, cutting up the greens. He arrived breathless, gave a remarkable address, and afterwards begged no one to betray the desecration of the greens to the inquiry that would certainly follow. But what did he *say*, when he was not making a fool of himself? What did he *say* that brought men clustering around on the dunes and on to the roof? She couldn't remember: it didn't seem to matter. It was just the man himself, somehow, his odd gaieties, his touching sadnesses. After the war, in the sombre peace, when the sometime V.A.D. married an ex-officer, they asked that Geoffrey should conduct the ceremony. "If," said the clergyman consulted, "you mean Studdert Kennedy I advise you to have someone in reserve. He will probably forget to turn up."

Without a doubt, he was fiercely disapproved of by many worthy people, so that it would be quite wrong to suppose that the personal memories of this time which have survived are all happy ones. He was widely held to be a mountebank. "Woodbine Willie: that impossible fellow! No use for him. Swears like a trooper: quite mad!" Such was a frequent opinion, as quoted by D. F. Carey. The swearing was common enough form; what made it notable in Geoffrey's case was his habit, which grew on him in these years, of doing so on platform and pulpit, as well as elsewhere. Thus it was reported how, when once two sardonic characters passed a hut labelled 'Vicarage', the one said to the other: "Bill, 'ere's the bloody Vicarage." Geoffrey immediately emerged to say: "Right! And here's the bloody Vicar!"

Perhaps it was true. The swearing in general is an

accepted fact, though it has to be remembered it would probably be considered more noteworthy then than now. The habit of sitting on the ledge of a pulpit, with legs astride would, however, possibly be regarded as interesting even yet. But as to the swearing, Colonel R. B. Campbell, of the 4th Army Infantry School, remembered the effect of Geoffrey's going on to the stage, at his first arriving there, with the words: "I know what you're thinking: here comes the bloody parson." The effect was considerable; but not so considerable as the splendid words which followed, and that from a man ill and worn at the time. But such habits did not endear him to everyone.

There was an occasion when they brought him to serious trouble. It happened in the winter of 1918. The Second Army, under the command of General Plumer, was stationed in and around Cologne. Now Plumer, he whose puffed cheeks and white moustache peer out from photographs of that old-time war, was, it appears, a devout person. It was reported of him, indeed, that on the night before the blowing of the mines under the Messines Ridge, he was observed to be at prayer. As the moment approached, for which so long grim tunnellers under the ridge had prepared, as birds began twittering in the dawn while thousands of troops waited in silence, an aide, wishing to borrow some night-glasses, entered the General's bedroom. He found his chief kneeling by the bedside. But now the moment was near. Silently, the staff officer picked up the glasses, and trained them out on to the distant line. Dead on time, the mines blew, and the sound of gunfire followed the cataclysmic roar. The General continued his prayers.

Perhaps such stern and soldierly piety was not likely to be sympathetic to such wildly unconventional Christianity as Geoffrey's. However, there the General, now a victorious one, was at the great parade service in Cologne. The preacher was Geoffrey. What followed is told by one who was present:

"S.K. was grossly misunderstood. Apart from the fact that he was at that time under the impression that the soldiers understood only three universal adjectives, the pattern of his sermon was apparently the building-up of an Aunt Sally which he then proceeded to knock down. The Aunt Sally in question was the soldiers' mistaken idea of God. Unfortunately, the General did not grasp the idea, and was throughout under the impression that what S.K. was pouring out was his own conception of the Almighty. He became so shocked and incensed that he did not hear the end."[1]

Geoffrey found himself reported to the Assistant Chaplain General in Cologne. With the report went the request that the Second Army be purged forthwith of such a heretic. The order was obeyed, and the offender, at the height of his fame, sent down to the base at Havre. A more immediate consequence was an encounter with a staff officer at the station after the disaster.

"Are you the fellow who preached this morning?"

"I have that honour."

"Well, all I can say is, you ought to be cashiered or locked up in an asylum."

True, they then travelled together amicably. Many people found it difficult to be angry with Geoffrey for long. But that detail does not affect the heart of the matter. The question remains as to why he conducted himself in this way at all. It was certainly damaging, not least in that his eccentricities tended to figure so largely in his popular reputation. Maybe the answer is to be found in another direction al-

[1] Private information.

together—in the tensions which can arise in a profoundly religious man from the struggle to square what he believes of the loving kindness of God, with the squalid horrors of a world said, incredibly enough, to be His.

"Now do you understand, you miserable little parson, with your petty shibboleths, this is the real thing, War!" So he imagined the shells shrieking to him as they passed overhead in the preliminary bombardment on the Somme. And when he returned with the Military Cross from the business on the ridge at Messines in 1917 and met Carey, Geoffrey said: "You know, this business has made me less cocksure of much of which I was cocksure before. On two points I am certain: Christ and his Sacrament. Apart from that I am not certain of anything."

But such tormenting uncertainties do not afflict everyone. There are always some who can find no difficulties at all in the idea of prayer before Messines or in reciting the 'Our Father' before take-off in the aircraft which carried the bomb to Hiroshima. What is more, they are often persons of much Christian devotion. There are others, again in any age, to whom the whole thing is an offence to the intelligence, just as there are some again to whom it is hypocrisy. And always, inevitably, there is the majority to whom the subject is a matter of indifference. In the centre of them all, coldly blown upon by every wind of opinion, is the man who exposes his own belief to them all and yet strives to keep it warm and living. Such an one was Geoffrey.

The war, blasting away many of his preconceptions, forced upon him the task of sorting the true from the false in the resulting wreckage. What, for instance, did one make of it when one day one bent over a boy at Communion with the words "—preserve thy body and soul unto everlasting life", and the next day came upon the boy's body obscenely shattered? What was the purpose of prayer in such circumstances? What was the good of it all, in any circumstances? Who and what was this God whom custom comfortably called Almighty, and what was he playing at? How came it that some of the bravest and best had often no time for religion whatever? Above all, how did Christ fit into this picture? Did his words really hold water? And what was the inner relationship, if any, between the shattered boy and the Cross with the broken body on it?

There were various ways of dealing with such awkward questions, of course. One was to be genuinely unaware that they existed. Another was to be aware, but to rely upon the tough hide of institutional religion to turn aside such shafts. A third was to face them. Geoffrey chose the third. The result was to draw from him memorable answers, "the ruminations of an incurably religious man under battle conditions" as he once called them, to many of the questions which vexed then, and certainly vex now, a great many people of good will who look with inquiring eyes from the outside upon the Church and all its doings.

It was the consuming desire to get alongside such people, to talk their language, to think their thoughts, and yet commend his God to them which made Geoffrey act and speak so unconventionally, even shockingly. He wanted to shock, for doing so served the double purpose of capturing the attention of the indifferent and disassociating his message from the pasteboard Christ who, it seemed to him, was too often offered by his official representatives. For this his hatred was enormous. It was a falsity he was constantly attacking, as in the bitter verse he called *A Sermon*.

My brethren, the ways of God
No man can understand.
We can but wait in awe and watch
The wonders of his hand.
O weeping mother torn with grief
Poor stricken heart that cries,
And rocks a cradle empty now,
Tis by God's will he dies . . .

"When the war broke out," he wrote in *The Hardest
Part*, "there was a regular run upon the bank of God,
and our churches were thronged with distracted people
waving cheques for protection duly endorsed 'Through
Jesus Christ Our Lord.' They soon got sick of it, of
course, and fell away. In a dim way they realised it
was useless . . . A chaplain said to me the other day;
'Don't discourage last-resort religion: it is better than
none at all.' I don't agree. It's worse than no religion.
It's a base form of idolatry."

Such language did not appeal to all. But it meant a
great deal to the only kind of people he really cared
about, the ordinary men who, in their tens of thousands were bearing the heat and burden of that terrible
day. These were they who gave him his famous name.
How it came, no one seems to know.

It emerged, and became universal. "Has Captain
Kennedy gone along?" an officer looking for Geoffrey
once asked of a sentry.

"No, sir."

"Have you seen the Chaplain, then?"

"No, sir."

"Have you had the padre this way?"

"No, sir."

"Look," said the officer, "have you seen Woodbine
Willie lately?"

"Yes, sir: just gone by."

After the war, it was suggested to Geoffrey that he should drop the use of this curious title. He declined, being very proud of it, having once written:

> They gave me this name like their nature
> Compacted of laughter and tears,
> A sweet that was born of the bitter
> A joke that was torn from the years.

But it took some earning, and it was not to be earned only with words. Here, as always, what he was and did is inextricably bound up with what he said. What he said is important now, and always will be in a world where suffering and death lie just beneath the surface of things, however well concealed. Yet to find this message it is necessary to seek it among the circumstances that gave it birth.

An encounter which took place in a hut at the base at Etaples, between Geoffrey and another remarkable man towards the end of 1916, is as good a starting point as any.

CHAPTER IV

THE MESSAGE OF WOODBINE WILLIE

THE OCCASION of the encounter was the arrival at the base at Etaples of a diffident clergyman of a type familiar among the character parts in the Anglican *dramatis personae* of any generation—the schoolmaster-parson. This was a certain Theodore Bayley Hardy, sometime grammar-school headmaster, at the time of his meeting with Geoffrey, vicar of the country parish of Hutton Roof, Kirby Lonsdale. He had wanted very much to be a chaplain; all his quiet life he had known intuitions of some tremendous experience awaiting him. But in 1916 he was over fifty so that there had been difficulties. However, there he was in Etaples at last, wondering quite what to do next. In these circumstances he was advised to see "a certain Mr. Studdert Kennedy, now so famous, who had by the magic of his personality got at the heart and mind of men".[1] This, it may be noted, was when Geoffrey had himself been in France less than a year.

The meeting which followed was a memorable one. "It was held in an ordinary office room; but in that room was significance, that wild thing that leaps out from unexpected places; an ordinary hour, a period of time; but the light of the ladder pitched between Heaven and Charing Cross shone on the faces of the two as they talked."[2] So wrote the biographer of Hardy. The words are mysterious; but they indicate at least something of the kind of person Geoffrey had become by this time; a man of compelling influence and power for the most part quite unconscious of either. The proof lies in the kind of padre Hardy himself became. That old war, nor its successor, never produced a greater than this gentle priest of fantastic heroism; the oldest man, from that day to this, ever to receive the supreme decoration. And the beginning of it was in the inspiration of this one meeting in the Assistant Chaplain General's office at Etaples.

"I remember the conversation very well," Geoffrey wrote. "He asked me to tell him the best way of working. I said: 'Live with the men; go everywhere they go. Make up your mind you will share all their risks, and more if you can do any good. The line is the key to the whole business. Work in the very front, and they will listen to you; but if you stay behind, you're wasting your time. Men will forgive you anything but lack of courage and devotion.'"

[1] M. Hardy: *Hardy, V. C.* Skeffington.
[2] ibid.

76

"I remember walking up and down saying this very fiercely, because I was full of it. He took it so humbly and eagerly that I was ashamed of myself, and loved him. I said the more padres died in battle doing Christian deeds the better; most of us would be more useful dead than alive. He asked me about purely spiritual work. I said: 'There is very little; it is all muddled and mixed. Take a box of fags in your haversack and a great deal of love in your heart, and go up to them: laugh with them, joke with them. You can pray with them sometimes; but pray for them always.' I felt he would be able to do it all much better than I, because he had the power that belongs to saints, and I was such an ordinary man. I told him some yarns, and we both laughed over them. We shook hands. I have never seen him since. If I did influence him, it is just another instance of the queer instruments God can use."[1]

Hardy went out to an extraordinary career. Yet of all the critics who so fiercely assailed the Anglican Chaplains of the first war only C. E. Montague seems ever to have heard of him. "There was the hero and saint, T. B. Hardy, to whom a consuming passion of human brotherhood brought, as well as rarer things, the M.C., the D.S.O., the V.C., the unaccepted invitation of the King to come home as one of his own chaplains and live, and then the death which everyone had seen to be certain."[2] That is all, and that is a pity, for in Hardy so many of the failures of others seem somehow redeemed and forgiven. If, as some maintain, the scenes of that ancient conflict are still visited by the ghosts of those who took part in them—and to stand by the Menin Gate on a winter evening with all those names yet crying from the

[1] ibid.
[2] C. E. Montague: *Disenchantment.*

walls in the fading light, or on the Vimy Ridge on a
summer day, with the tourist traffic unconcernedly
humming by at a distance, is to find it easy enough
to believe—then Hardy's will be amongst them. Hardy
inquiring, as one staff officer remembered him, when
all was mud and fog and poisoned scum filling every
shell-hole, "Pardon me; but could you kindly direct me
to the front line?" Or Hardy staying, as once he did,
for thirty-six hours by some unfortunate slowly sinking in the mud from which none could get him out.
Or Hardy, lost, and wandering hazardously back in
the dark from the wrong direction upon some trigger-
happy outpost. The 'end which all had seen to be
certain', the great experience of which, among his
boys, among his Westmorland hills, he had once
dreamed, came with a shot out of the dark as he
was crossing a plank bridge over the River Selle in
October 1918. His record ends briefly: "Died of
wounds (gunshot) received in action." Three months
before, he had written, in a letter to the Assistant
Chaplain General, thanking him humbly for certain
kind words about his V.C.; "Are you likely to meet
or write to Studdert Kennedy soon? If so, will you
tell him that I have often wished I could thank him
properly for that hour in your office which, more than
any other in my life, has helped me in this work.
You can understand how I feel about these ribbons
when I think of him."

Meanwhile, that queer instrument of God's purposes
had himself gone out from the room in Etaples to an
extraordinary career. Yet the bare records of what,
outwardly, happened to Geoffrey give no indication at
all of the terrific inner conflict of those years. It is
necessary to search elsewhere for the voice which still
speaks from out of the midst of it all. Even so, the
records have their significance, if only in showing a

characteristic mode of conduct much more in evidence then than now of concealing, alike from the public as from the domestic eye, what was really going on. The serving soldier of 1914–18 knew as much about the horrors of wars as Goya, probably more. But at the time he does not seem to have been in the habit of talking about them. Indeed, the curtain was not really lifted until the war literature of a decade afterwards. But while it was all happening the participant in the horrors of the Somme and Passchendaele and the like preferred to keep his mouth shut before noncombatants, much as a man who has seen a ghastly accident does not, in general, go into details at home about what the victims looked like. There was, in fact, 'a conspiracy of silence' as John Oxenham put it, and one of the many criticisms levelled against some of Geoffrey's writings of this time was that he broke it by revealing something of what he had seen. Later generations, of course, have been less inhibited, though whether as a result of a broadening of mind or of a coarsening of taste it would, perhaps, be difficult to say.

If, however, Geoffrey was too frank for some in his writings, his letters home show no lifting of the curtain on reality. They are naïve and simple: while the local press, at intervals faithfully reporting the remarks of the Vicar of St. Paul's on leave in his parish, presents a similar picture of a man deliberately confining himself to the outer surface of things: A few conventional sentiments, and a joke here and there. The conventional sentiments come as a surprise until it is realised that they were common currency of the day. It is remarkable, for instance, to find Geoffrey, in a letter home which he clearly thought might be his last, advising his wife as to the upbringing of their son in terms which spring almost ready-made from the world of Ernest Raymond's *Tell England*. "Make him a sportsman, encourage him to play games and play the game. Teach him to despise cowardice . . . Teach him that a gentleman should choose one of the poorly paid but honourable professions . . . Teach him to love and reverence women . . ."

It is puzzling that such an original thinker as Geoffrey, who spent so much of his time blasting out of their complacency people who lived by such fatuous concepts in the religious as in the social field, should himself have appeared to subscribe to them. It is also interesting, as indicative of the values of a culture not even yet, after all this time, quite dead. Perhaps it never dies; but only fades away, like the old soldier. Certainly, no true picture of Geoffrey, nor any appreciation of the distance he had to travel in drawing away from these ideas is possible, unless it is understood how once he accepted them.

Only when some of his letters of this time, some yellowing newspaper cuttings, some hints from his official record are put together and fitted into the enormous tapestry, full of violent death, and battle scenes, of the historical background, does some little of the truth of what really happened to him begin to emerge. For instance, in 1916; to his wife:

"My own darling Em,

I have had rather a sharp attack of asthma which is now over. How I wish I could see the last of it. I have succeeded in throwing this off more quickly and I must be glad of that. But it takes me more suddenly now and hurts more than it did. I don't know quite what to make of it—"

He never did discover what to make of it, except to say that it made him feel 'like a rat pulled by its tail though a hedge on a wet morning'. The affliction plagued him constantly until the end, and is mentioned often enough in his medical records as to make plain that for much of his time in France, which was not the best place for a delicate man, he was ailing. 'Debility' and 'Trench Fever' also occur. And the source of the memorable lung-tearing cough which so many heard in aftertimes is probably indicated in the entry 'gas-poisoning'.

Perhaps that happened on some fearful occasion just hinted at in another letter:

"I have been up the line again. We got deluged with gas shells and had a very terrible time. I got a bit of gas, which makes me feel very miserable: sore throat, running nose, aching eyes. Tomorrow there is a fight, I believe. By the time you get this it will all be over and done with. I am writing this on the eve of it, wondering whether I shall be safe when I write again. One can't help wondering, though I am not anxious—."

He may not have been anxious; but he was often enough terrified, distraught and miserable, no doubt with many others. But little enough of the reality of what he was saying and feeling comes through reports he gave, sometimes in written messages which were read from the pulpit in St. Paul's, sometimes in person when on leave. There was this, for instance, after the Somme:

"The Vicar first explained why his despatches, which he sent from time to time, have ceased. His experiences were so awful that, if he had written home about them, he would have frightened everyone to death. It was difficult to describe life there without giving the impression that it could scarcely be possible for anyone to come back alive . . . The officers seemed bored at first at the idea of having a clergyman with them. They seemed to assume he would stay behind, keep out of danger, and bury the dead. He had to make them feel differently. But the men gave him a good reception. Burying the dead was very unpleasant sometimes. In some cases he had to bury them where they lay, lying on his stomach in the dark to say the service . . . The work he was doing was being done by all the padres . . ."

Or this grim picture, later that same year;

"We always have a service before a trench raid, the fellows in tin hats, hands and faces blackened. I always go up with the men to a raid, and this has tightened the bond between them and me enormously. If you get men into such a state that they will ask for a service, you have hold of them—"

Or again, this; after that fighting at Messines, before which General Plumer had said his prayers;

"He told them how a large shell dropped just behind him, when he had his arms full of wooden stakes. When he heard the noise he cried 'Lord, help us', dropped the stakes, and fell flat on his face. His companion turned round and said, 'You've got the wind up!' Then there came heavy fighting in which he was engaged in tending the wounded. In one engagement the supply of morphia at a dressing station had given out, and he volunteered to fetch some. 'After that,' he added, 'I was rung up on the telephone and told I had ten days' leave and the M.C.' "

The *London Gazette* for August 16th, 1917, put it differently :

"For conspicuous gallantry and devotion to duty. He showed the greatest courage and disregard of his own safety in attending wounded under heavy fire. He searched shell-holes for our own and enemy wounded, assisting them to the dressing station, and his cheerfulness and endurance had a splendid effect upon all ranks, whom he constantly visited."

Perhaps there was little at all exceptional in any of it. And more expert hands painted in after-times infinitely more graphic pictures of what the squalid and murderous war was for the combatant, living and dying in those fantastic slits in the ground which stretched for years from Ostend to Switzerland. Answering the question, "What was it like?" Robert Graves, forty years later, called the trenches "our homes, our privies, our graveyards; like air-raid shelters hastily dug in a muddy field, fenced by a tangle of rusty wire, surrounded by enormous craters, subjected not only to an incessant air-raid of varying intensity, but to constant surprise attacks by professional killers, and without any protection against flooding in times of rain."

And the smells: of corpses, latrine-buckets, rotting sandbags, human sweat, chloride of lime, frying bacon. And the sounds; clatter of working-parties, rattle of dixie-lids, squeak of rats; laughter, curses and, at sunrise and sunset the cry of 'stand-to'.[1]

Geoffrey's picture of the muttered service for luckless ones setting off on that singularly appalling enterprise, the trench raid, takes on a more sombre colouring in Sassoon's account of just such an event: "It was now midnight. The fire parties had vanished into the darkness on all fours. It was raining quietly and persistently. An occasional flare revealed the streaming rain, blanched the tangles of wire that wound away into the gloom and came to nothing, bringing down the night." Later, when the survivors returned, "Among them was a grey-haired lance corporal, who had one of his feet almost blown off . . . He said; 'Thank God Almighty for this; I've been waiting eighteen months for it, and now I can go home'."[2]

[1] *Sunday Times.* November 9th, 1958.
[2] Siegfried Sassoon: *Memoirs of an Infantry Officer.* Faber & Faber.

Such reportage was far beyond Geoffrey's powers. It recreates something of the feel of the darkened world in which he, with so many others, was living. But what remains to be accounted for is the extraordinary fame which, even by the time of his meeting with Hardy, had begun to gather about him.

The beginning of that starts in a small way with a press-cutting of 1916. Once again he is reporting back to the people at St. Paul's.

"When I left you at the end of last October I got a notice saying I was being withdrawn from my battalion in order to preach the National Mission. I was very much cut up at going away to a soft job. I reported to the headquarters of the Chaplains' department and saw Bishop Gwynne and poured out all my dissatisfaction. He heard me out, and then said; 'It doesn't matter what you want. As you have been given by the Lord Almighty the gift of the gab you have to do as you are told.' He said I was not much good except for talking. So for ten days I preached three times a day to an audience varying from 500 to 1,500 but before the proceedings ended I had an attack of the 'go wrong with my wind-box' (Laughter.) My temperature rose to 103, and between the wheezes I preached."

What actually happened followed the pattern which became familiar to those who helplessly watched him killing himself in the decade after the war. He would become possessed, after the uncomfortable, disturbing way of the prophets of old, whom some thought mad. It was a process Geoffrey himself hated and feared; but while he was thus the words poured from him with incredible force, every sentence loaded; the style novel, the manner unforgettable. And then at the end of it he would be left shaken and exhausted. All those words, all that matchless eloquence, has long vanished into the indifferent air. It is possible to grasp something of its power only by observing its effect on him and its impact on others.

Its effect on him was to put him in hospital, gasping for breath. He was there several weeks. When he emerged he was sent to paradise in the South of France. And then, at the beginning of the great frost of the winter of 1916, he can be found moving north again to the bleak land of the armies where in that season corpses left in the open were before long iron hard and where not a few men died in some freezing listening-post, by night, in the phenomenal cold. Fourteen hours to cover forty-two miles, in twenty-two degrees of frost, in a train without a door was Geoffrey's minor share in these discomforts. He was on his way back to his own battalion, still under orders, ostensibly to preach the glad tidings of this National Mission, actually to deliver himself yet further of the message which was shaking him. Thence he was sent back to the Channel coast where, among their mountains of stores, the dockers and the transport people lived. And after that he passed through all the great bases behind the lines, wandering on like some novel kind of prophet who, unlike any of his predecessors, considered it as important to make his hearers laugh as well as listen. "He didn't know," according to the faithful local paper, "whether he touched their souls. But he touched their sense of humour. They split their sides laughing at him."

That was among troops and dockers. The next stage was a grand tour among military high society; from brigadiers to brass-hats of the heaviest calibre whose very word, even when it was not a very intelligent word, determined the destinies of armies. Sassoon has an interesting picture of one such in *The General*.

'He's a cheery old card,' grunted Harry to Jack
As they slogged up to Arras with rifle and pack.
But he did for them both with his plan of attack.[1]

It would be interesting indeed to know what these potentates with their attendant retinues made of the Irish padre sent amongst them. The mind quails before the difficulties inherent in the enterprise. However, they treated him with much distinction, which he found very frightening. They also, as he told the people at St. Paul's, gave him a splendid horse, which threw him the second time he got into the saddle. Yet apparently something of what he said got through, since it was not long afterwards, at one of the infantry schools to which he was posted, that the Commander of one of the Armies sent for him. They were together two hours, while the rest of the establishment marvelled, like the people of Israel during the absence of Moses on Sinai, at this extreme sign of divine favour.

On the whole, however, he was more than glad to claim from the Assistant Chaplain General permission to return whence he had come. By the autumn of 1917, therefore, he was back in the line.

But meanwhile he had begun to write, and this, as far as his wider fame was concerned, was the beginning of things. It began by chance, in a manner described by a fellow padre, Frederick Macnutt, later Canon of Canterbury, who also was involved in the Mission. In the February of 1917 this man was at Boulogne where he met "An Irishman charming, amusing and eloquent. He was known in the line as Woodbine Willie. I never knew anyone with such power . . . We met every morning and talked over our message. One day I quoted some poetry to him, and he told me 'he did

[1] Siegfried Sassoon: *Collected Poems 1908–1956*. Faber & Faber.

a lot of the poetry stunt'. I suggested he should write a poem for the men on the National Mission. The next day he brought me the result . . ."

This was *A Sermon in a Billet*, the beginning of Geoffrey's dialect poems.

> Our Padre says I'm a sinner, and John Bull says I'm a saint,
> And both of 'em's sure to be liars, for I'm neither of 'em, I ain't;
> I'm a man, an' a man's a mixture, right from 'is very birth,
> For part of 'im comes from 'eaven, and part of 'im comes from earth.
> There's nothing in man that's perfect, and nothing that's all complete,
> He's nobbut a big beginning, from 'is 'ead to the soles of 'is feet.

No one would be likely to claim, and Geoffrey himself never did, any literary or artistic merit whatever for this kind of thing. But there is at least one reason why his verse in general, and these early dialect poems in particular, is not lightly to be dismissed. It represents a break-through in the age-long problem of communication—a problem of quite critical importance which needs to be solved in every generation by any who have, or believe themselves to have, a body of truth to communicate.

Obviously, the language in which the broad truths of religion can be communicated to the mass of the people varies from age to age. Nobody appears in the present, for instance, to have found the secret as regards the millions of secondary-modern educated citizenry with its television background. And certainly Geoffrey's dialect verses would scarcely have meant much to the more sophisticated soldiery of the second world war. But the men he had in mind and heart were of a very different sort, for the most part the simple working-men of pre-1914 Britain, the kind of people he had known so well and loved so much in the back streets of Leeds and Rugby and Worcester. That they were men in uniform did not alter their essential nature. The dialect he used was truly their speech. The sentimentality was truly of their very being. Not surprisingly, the *Rough Rhymes* as he called them, swept through the armies in France and the people at home like a fire; burning some; warming many. His favourite, ever recurring theme of the involvement of God in the sufferings of mankind comes out in one of the earliest of these verses, *The Sorrows of God*.

I wonder if that's what it really means,
That figure what 'angs on the Cross.
I remember I seed one the other day
As I stood with the Captain's 'oss . . .
Well, what if 'e came to the earth today,
Came walking about this trench,
'Ow 'is 'eart would bleed for the sights 'e seed
I' the mud and the blood and the stench.
And I guess it would finish 'im up for good
When 'e came to this old sap end,
And 'e seed that bundle o' nothen there,
For 'e wept at the grave uv 'is friend.

It was a long time indeed since spiritual insight had come in this workaday form; and longer still since any cleric had so abandoned the customary reticences as to mention matters on the whole much more firmly left unsaid then than now:

I met 'er one night down in Leicester Square,
With paint on 'er lips and dye on 'er 'air.
With 'er fixed glad eye and 'er brazen stare —
She were a gal on the streets.

So the leave-expired man in that old wartime London goes with her to the usual sleazy room. There, he chances to mention the name of a comrade who had also, apparently, in his time been to that same place. He adds that he is dead.

> She stood there and swayed like a drunken man
> And 'er face went green where 'er paint began
> Then she muttered, 'My Gawd, I can't' and ran—
> She were a gal on the streets.

"Verily I say unto you," quotes the text italicised at the head of these lines, "the harlots go into the Kingdom of Heaven before you."

It was all most uncomfortable, most startling. And yet it was incredibly satisfying to the many who had longed to be able to see where, if at all, Christ was to be found in the horrors which had come upon the world. The answer appeared to be that he was to be found in the most unexpected places:

> Easy does it—bit o' trench 'ere
> Mind that blinkin' bit o' wire,
> There's a shell 'ole on your left there,
> Lift 'im up a little 'igher . . .
> 'Ere we are now, stretcher-case, boys,
> Bring 'im aht a cup o' tea!
> *Inasmuch as ye have done it*
> *Ye have done it unto me.*

And counterbalancing this was the deep sense of guilt, inexpugnable as the blood on Lady Macbeth's hands, which lay on many a simple soul by reason of the dark deeds war and his betters had forced upon him. So the casualty awaiting the doctor ruminates:

> Well, I've done my bit o' scrappin'
> And I've done it quite a lot;
> Nicked 'em neatly wiv my bayonet

> So I needn't waste a shot.
> 'Twas my duty, and I done it,
> But I 'opes the doctor's quick,
> For I wish I 'adn't done it:
> Gawd! it turns me shamed and sick.

This sort of thing was listened to because it was real. And it was real because the writer could get inside the carefully guarded door behind which the inarticulate kept their deepest feelings. Nobody else was writing for the inarticulate; nobody else ever did. Nobody since his time has done, which is a sobering thought. And what was he trying to say? The outlines of a message later far more carefully worked-out and written for a different audience altogether are nonetheless to be found in some of these early dialect pieces. The purpose is always the same—to try to make sense to the ordinary man of some of the incomprehensible things religious people, especially parsons, when encountered in the form of the occasional army chaplain, were in the habit of saying to him. The contradictions, in Geoffrey's passionately held opinion, between the harsh facts of life and the current presentation of religion, bothered the average man far more than was generally realised. That which appeared to be plainly untrue was naturally written off as nonsense. A first need, therefore, was to make that which was true appear true. Thus several of these longer pieces begin with a statement of bewilderment and go on to try and replace it by meaning.

The question of Judgment: for instance.

> Our Padre were a solemn bloke
> We called 'im dismal Jim.
> It fairly gave ye bloomin' creeps
> To sit and 'ark at 'im,
> When 'e were on wi' Judgment Day

> Abaht that great white throne,
> And 'ow each chap would 'ave to stand
> And answer on 'is own.
> And if 'e tried to chance 'is arm,
> And 'ide a single sin,
> There'd be the angel Gabriel,
> Wi' books to do 'im in—

Did in fact any parson ever say any such thing? Possibly not. What mattered was that he was thought to do so. And that matters still, half a century later, when by very many he is still thought to be uttering the same enormities.

However, it is of little use to remove a misconception without replacing it with something better. And so Geoffrey in these verses—quoted time and oft by a post-war generation until the memory gradually faded —goes on to create a picture of a personal, Everyman's judgment at once understandable and haunting. The speaker, here as elsewhere imagined as some homespun philosopher yarning to his pals, tells how he dreamed a dream of himself, dead, and standing by some solemn sea.

> Its waves they got in my inside
> And touched my memory,
> And day by day and year by year
> My life came back to me
> I seed just what I were, and what
> I'd 'ad the chance to be . . .

So he stands there until, after an age, a figure comes to look down at him. This figure has a most remarkable face.

> It never changed yet always changed
> Like the sea beneath the sun.
> 'Twere all men's face yet no man's face

91

> And a face no man can see—
> All eyes were in his eyes—all eyes,
> My wife's, and a million more
> And once I thought as those two eyes
> Were the eyes of the London whore . . .

There is no court of judgment, no white throne.
Only this figure beside that queer, moaning sea. And
when at last the figure speaks it is to utter only one
word; "Well—?" Yet somehow the word is so loaded
with sorrowful accusation that there seems nothing
left to do but to ask immediately for the punishments
of hell itself. But the request is not granted:

> . . . that 'Ell is for the blind
> And not for those that see.
> You know that you have earned it lad,
> So you must follow me.
> Follow me on the paths of pain
> Seeking what you have seen,
> Until at last you can build the 'Is'
> With the bricks of 'Might 'ave been'.

Of course, it is confused. Anyone could pick holes
in it; anyone could ask what exactly 'seeking what
you have seen' is supposed to mean, or what is the
nature of the 'Is' which is to be built out of the ruins
of a man's past. But equally critical—and equally
useless—questions could be asked about much of the
language of eschatology. The Four Last Things: Death,
Heaven, Hell and the Judgment do not lend themselves to precise statement, being concepts to be
grasped as much by the emotions as by the intellect.
And here, in these verses, was a novel breakthrough
on the level of emotional understanding. Geoffrey's
dialect poems, thus written to meet the need of getting across something of the message of the National

Mission, were an immense success, no only in that context, but far beyond it.

Their derivation is obvious. Anyone who cares to compare Geoffrey's —

> Yes, I'm fighting for old England
> And for eighteenpence a day,
> And I'm fighting like an 'ero
> So the daily papers say . . .
> > *with*
> My name is O'Kelly, I've heard the Revelly
> From Birr to Bareilly, from Leeds to Lahore

—will catch the similarities, of vocabulary and style with Kipling's *Barrack Room Ballads.* There was the great original which Geoffrey took as his model. What is more, the man he was speaking for was the direct descendant of Kipling's Tommy Atkins. Not so many years separated the old British Regular Army with its horse-lines, its leathery N.C.O.s, its vocabulary spattered with Hindustani words like *blighty* and *cushy,* from the vast citizen army which fought the first war in France and Flanders. Indeed, they often intermingled; the old army taught the new before it eventually perished at the early battles of Ypres. Many a recruit to Kitchener's Armies encountered in the course of his training men who were the spitting images of those whose hoarse voices mutter from the pages of *Barrack Room Ballads.* The worldly-wise sergeant mentioned by Montague in *Disenchantment* whose idea of a route-march was to conduct his charges to the nearest pub, there himself to sit enthroned while they bought his drinks, might be the very man celebrated in Kipling's *The Sergeant's Wedding.* Consider also Kipling's ranker-philosopher who, as on some calm evening his troopship crosses the Indian Ocean, meditates on life:

93

For to admire and for to see
For to be'old this world so wide—
It never done no good to me
But I can't drop it if I tried.

This very man seems to speak again in Geoffrey's;

I've tramped the whole world over
Through 'Frisco back to Dover
And I know my 'uman nature through and through.

The difference is that in this latter case the subject
of the meditation, strangely enough, is the Cross,
and how much courage—here saluted by a connois-
seur of a wandering life's many and varied brutalities
—must have been required of Christ not only to endure that exquisite torture; but to forgive its inflictors.

Similarly, it is not immediately apparent that the
thoughts troubling the man surprised by gas while
sitting quietly in his trench in *Thy Will Be Done* are
to be concerned with prayer and the answer:

I were sittin' me down on my 'unkers
And 'avin a pull at my pipe,
And larfin like fun at a blind old 'un,
What were 'avin a try to snipe.

Suddenly, into this placid scene there breaks the
ghastly sound, a true period piece, of the 'Strombo',
a gas-alarm operated by beating with a bar upon an
empty shell-case. And when the philosopher springs
to his feet he sees the yellow cloud drifting across
towards his parapet. Like Shakespeare's Mariner on
his sinking ship in the opening scene of *The Tempest*
he turns in his extremity to prayer, that the wind may
be changed. After all, he had been told often enough
that prayer was a certain winner, if backed by something called faith. So he prays. But the wind does not
shift; the gas cloud comes inexorably on, and the poem

94

finds him meditating in verse and in hospital on yet another mystery of religion. He finds the answer in a 'story' he has been reading, presumably in one of the soldiers' New Testaments handed out in quantities in those times by the well-meaning. The story turns out to be Gethsemane:

> 'E prayed to the Lord, and 'e sweated blood,
> And yet 'e were crucified—

But at least the Christ of the Garden was given the power to see through to the bitter end that which he had felt called to do. So it is always with prayer which is truly Christian. Unfortunately, it so rarely is in practice, a fact which Geoffrey, in these times and afterwards, never tired of stating. Thus, in *The Hardest Part*:

"Too often we model our prayers upon the false interpretation of Gethsemane. Our prayers are too often either a wail of agony or a kind of indent upon God for supplies to meet our needs, with 'Thy Will be done' put in at the end in case God cannot take away the pain or grant us the supplies, 'Thy Will be done' ceases to be the great prayer, and becomes the necessary apology for praying. It becomes an act of passive submission instead of an act of positive and powerful aspiration . . . We have taught people to use prayer too much as a means of comfort . . . the comfort of the cushion, not the comfort of the Cross. Because we have failed in prayer to bear the Cross, we have also failed to win the crown."

And that, of course, is as true now as ever. The trouble is that it is so tough a truth that not many will ever want to have much to do with it. Geoffrey, in saying these things, often resented, was certainly being true to his prophet's vocation. For that, after all, is not to popularise religion; but to make plain the truth about religion. And that usually involves saying things which comes strangely upon ears unaccustomed to such starkness. So the quivering intensity of his final definition of prayer, surely one of the most splendid ever written, makes a nonsense of much which commonly goes under that name: "Prayer is the means of communication by which the suffering and triumphant God meets his band of volunteers and pours his spirit into them, and sends them out to fight, to suffer, and to conquer in the end."

The Rough Rhymes made a big impact. A letter of Geoffrey's to his wife, in the February of 1918 from the Fourth Army Infantry School at Flixecourt, might be taken as his final word on them. "I got my presentation copies of the *Rough Rhymes* this morning and sold them all in about ten minutes for about twice their proper price. So much more for the fund—"

The 'fund' was St. Dunstan's. Geoffrey's handing over the whole of the proceeds from his enormously successful book to that admirable organisation for the blind was merely a continuation of the kind of impulsive generosity which at Rugby had led him to give away his overcoat and at Worcester one of the family beds. But it was hard on the family, and continued for a while, understandably, to be a sore point domestically. It is doubtful whether he ever had much understanding of the earning power of his pen. He was a child in such matters, though fortunately a child with kindly guardians. Moore Ede, Dean of Worcester, drew the attention of Hodder & Stoughton to his work—sent to the Dean, apparently, from time to time in the humble hope he might be interested. The early contracts between Geoffrey and his publishers were all made out 'Care of the Deanery'. And thereafter his interests were looked after by Sir Ernest Hodder Williams.

This same letter in which he refers to the *Rough Rhymes* also indicates that he was at work on other verses. "I am enclosing two poems so I hope you won't be disappointed that all the fatness of the envelope isn't letter. I have now five poems for the new book, so I'm getting on." The 'new book' refers to a further and later collection of his verse. The habit once begun of 'having a go at the poetry stunt' as he put it to Macnutt in Boulogne, remained with him, and continued to the end. The dialect verses, largely written to meet the needs of the National Mission, form only a small part of that which he eventually produced in the war years, and which reached edition after edition, "saying for the soldiers the things they wanted to say for themselves", as his publishers put it, and bringing home the truth to those at home. And to the verse of the war years was added later that of the decade afterwards. Geoffrey's verse therefore falls into the the two parts of *War Rhymes* and *Peace Rhymes*, and in fact originally appeared under those titles. The final collection, containing all the poems which he himself wished to live, was *The Unutterable Beauty*.

But somehow that damaging word 'rhymes' used by him with characteristic modesty, has stuck. It is true that the dialect verse might fairly be thus labelled, and seen as perhaps little more than a novel, and in their day brilliantly successful, form of Christian apologetic. But these, in the final collection in *The Unutterable Beauty*, amount to only twenty in a total of a hundred and four poems. Yet their effect in forming the public image of Geoffrey as a man who wrote ephemeral verses was as unfortunate as the nickname Woodbine Willie to any assessment of him as a serious thinker. The fact is that he was far more; very, very much far more than a rhymster. He was a

poet: the seeds of it were in him from the beginning;
they were peeping out when people used to be startled in his curate days at Rugby, as Bishop Herbert
recalled, by the arresting beauty of the language in
some of his sermons. The agonies of the war brought
them painfully to bloom, poppies on the rim of a
crater. And in what years afterwards remained they
continued to flower from time to time in other places.
How the gift developed in him during the war years
can best be seen by comparing the power of his
bitter lines on the Treaty of Versailles in *Dead and
Buried* with the naïvety of some of the dialect verse.

Yet that word could not be fairly used of his other
War Rhymes. Some of his best work is here; some of
his longest remembered; some of his least perishable.
To turn the pages of it now is to experience at least
two emotions—a feeling that one is here drawing
nearer than at any other point to Geoffrey as he really
was; and an excitement at the power and originality
of the work. Yet the general effect is curiously sombre,
as though here were the poetic testament of a soul
continually racked by some inner, personal pain, pre-
sided over, as it were, by the ever-present image of a
crucified Christ, his dolorous body a constant reminder
of the involvement of God in the world's sorrows.

> If he could speak, that Victim torn and bleeding,
> Caught in his pain and nailed upon the Cross,
> Has he to give the comfort souls are needing?
> Could he destroy the bitterness of loss?

It is in this poem *The Suffering God*, that there is
to be found Geoffrey's major poetic statement of the
basic doctrine of his faith—the one concept which
for him made sense of the problem of suffering.
And here are to be found the famous lines, the key to
the whole philosophy of his life:

Peace does not mean the end of all our striving
Joy does not mean the drying of our tears;
Peace is the power that comes to souls arriving
Up to the light where God Himself appears.

And the same theme occurs yet again in *The Comrade God*. The war made it necessary for him to fight very hard for the faith he had, and this inner conflict is reflected in his verse *Faith*.

How do I know that God is good? I don't.
I gamble like a man. I bet my life
Upon one side in life's great war—

Similarly, in *If Jesus Never Lived*, he faces the possibility that Christ could have been a product of wistful human imagining, and meditates upon what the world would be without him. And sometimes faith went altogether, to be recaptured unexpectedly in a moment of joy.

I lost my Lord and sought him long
I journeyed far, and cried
His name to every wandering wind
But still my Lord did hide . . .
I sought him where the hermit kneels
And tells his beads of pain.
I found him with some children here
In this green Devon lane.

Even the very titles of the poems indicate this continuing element of inner struggle; such as *The Soul of Doubt*, with its strange beginning:

That's it. Doubt's very soul of doubt
Lies here. Is God just faith in God,
Or can God work his will without
Our human faith?

And *Truth's Betrayal*, and *Tragedy* have echoes of the same struggle. Yet all the time, cheerfulness keeps breaking in. Comedy and tragedy co-exist in the spiritual life as in the physical, and it was Geoffrey's acute awareness of this which made him one of God's clowns, in whom laughter and tears were always getting mixed up.

> I scorn the sun
> I con the books of years in bitter rage.
> I swear that faith in God is dead and done :
> But then I turn a page,
> And shake my sides in laughter at His fun.

So inward doubts, outward sorrows, the piercingly felt brutalities and horrors of the world pressed upon him hard, and from the pressure emerged his poetry. The horrors especially affected him deeply, and no aspect of the manifold beastliness of a war which abounded in such moved him more than the sexual licence to which it gave rise. The venereal disease casualties of that old war were phenomenal, and as a man who lived among men he knew it and saw it. In *Idols* he spoke about this memorably, and his words are as applicable, perhaps, to our own pornographic society as to his. The ancient Gods, he says, still have their power :

> Still Venus stands with swelling breasts
> And sidelong glancing eyes
> And lures lust-driven devotees
> To trust her when she lies . . .

And here again the ever-recurrent image of a beaten and mocked-at Christ appears, dragged in the train of a triumphant Venus for her especial pleasure.

Yet his picture of the world, as it emerges in the poems, is not all ugly. Beauty, as well as cheerfulness, keeps breaking in; and the loveliness of the natural world stirs him to thanksgiving as often as its man-made squalor moves him to tears. Those—and they are many—who found matter for displeasure in his so often dwelling upon the Christ of the *via dolorosa*, stumbling and derided on his way to the Cross seem, oddly enough, to have missed the point that the dying Christ was the necessary precursor to the risen and triumphant Christ. But Geoffrey knew it: and realised also that he had to go that way himself:

> Blessed are the eyes that see
> The agony of God,
> Blessed are the feet that tread
> The paths his feet have trod.
> Blessed are the souls that solve
> The paradox of pain,
> And find the path that, piercing it,
> Leads through to Peace again.

A letter home, again from the Fourth Army Infantry School, this time in the October of 1917, makes mention of another book he was busy with.

"My own darling,

Here I am settled for three weeks at least. I had rather a ghastly journey down in a cattle truck, but now that I have got here it is a splendid place . . . I think they will let me have one evening a week for lectures so that I will have some decent work to do. I will also be able to get on with my book, and get it finished . . . Here one is far away from the fighting, and cannot even hear the guns . . ."

Where and what was this 'splendid place'? Since he was at Infantry Schools for four separate and lengthy periods, each far longer than the three weeks the letter mentions, it is worth looking at the kind of scene where he spent so much of his time; his mind seething with impressions, questions, memories, agonies, from his latest tour in the line. At the Infantry

Schools he had the comparative leisure and quiet sufficient to get some of them, at least, down on to paper. So the places were important to him, though he nowhere attempts any description of one. Fortunately, however, Siegfried Sassoon does, so that anyone who cares to accompany Lieutenant Sherston, that former fox-hunting man, through the opening chapters of *Memoirs of an Infantry Officer* will arrive very soon at the place from which Geoffrey dated so many of his letters home—the Fourth Army Infantry School, Flixecourt.

It lay between Amiens and Abbeville, a clean little town thirty miles behind the line, so it is not surprising that Geoffrey says he could not there hear the guns. Parades and lectures filled the day, the latter not always on matters closely relevant to the realities of the mud and guts fighting thirty miles away. Thus a big-game hunter would lecture on the use of the telescopic sight, and the instructors rhapsodise on the virtues of open warfare. The motto of the Commandant was "always do your utmost", and in the mornings there was bird-song, and the bell tolling in a church-tower. Did Geoffrey ever meditate, one wonders, as Sassoon did, upon the multiplicity of regimental badges in the audiences at lectures; the lion, the lamb, the harp, the phoenix and crown? Sassoon was there before the Somme; Geoffrey afterwards. But the place was the same. And the 'Sandy-haired Highland Major' who lectured on 'The Spirit of the Bayonet', and the sinewy sergeant who gave horrific demonstrations of the use of that weapon bear a remarkable resemblance to the kind of group, called by Geoffrey 'The travelling circus' with which he used later to go on morale-building missions.

It is difficult, at this distance of time, to understand what exactly his function would be at these Infantry

Schools. It was at Fourth Army Infantry School that he met Colonel R. B. Campbell, with whom he formed a close friendship. Colonel Campbell wrote. "I was much impressed with his personality and fire, and induced him to come and speak at our service the following Sunday. He came to St. Pol, but owing to an attack of asthma could not take the service; but he spoke at a smoking concert given that evening to all manner of people who were living at St. Pol; civilians as well as soldiers. He asked me if he could speak for ten minutes, got up on the stage smoking a cigarette and commenced with the remark; 'I know what you're thinking: here comes a bloody parson'. But as he spoke he seemed to get hold of his audience more and more.[1]

It was in consequence of this meeting that Geoffrey joined Campbell's unit at Hardelot, already mentioned, and began his travels with the 'circus', of which the boxer Jimmy Driscoll, was a member. Geoffrey would spar with the champion before intrigued audiences of troops, and later himself demonstrate unarmed combat. It appears fantastic, and no doubt was. Possibly it was intended to be, for here again was Geoffrey as the clown, totally disguising the breaking heart, which the poems reveal as he tumbled in the ring. He could be genuinely ridiculous, sometimes unconsciously. Campbell, it appears, was a keen egg-collector, and instructed his padre in the technique. He observed, however, one day when lecturing in the open, that the attention of his audience was markedly distracted by strange movements in the surrounding grass. It was Geoffrey, looking for nests.

But, as always, there was another side to the coin. On taking Geoffrey as chaplain to Hardelot Campbell had made the condition that there were to be no

[1] *G. A. Studdert Kennedy: By His Friends.*

parade services, and that if he could not attract men voluntarily to his services, he would be got rid of promptly. The result was those odd scenes around the church hut, which the V.A.D. nurse witnessed from a distance, the dunes around dotted with men who had failed to get in, and others on the roof trying to hear, through open windows, what Geoffrey was saying. "Never once," Campbell said, "did he fail to hold their attention, and inspire them with the big things of life. He was a man with a wonderful insight into character, and I never met one who was more fearless. He would box anybody, he would ride any horse, and he would face any General who attempted to criticise him and his methods." It was not only Generals who did so. There was a certain kind of officer, Campbell remembered, who was much offended, as Plumer was, by his unconventional manner. But others were not, and perhaps the extreme limit of his powers of attraction was reached when he succeeded in getting Australians, those formidable and unforgiving characters of the Western front, to listen to him.

The book which Geoffrey said his being at the Fourth Army Infantry School would enable him to get on with was *The Hardest Part*. Moore Ede went so far as to say it represented the attempt of 'an earnest man to do for the British soldier what the writer of the book of Job and the prophet Isaiah endeavoured to do for the men of their times'. The praise seems at the same time too lavish and too limiting: the book is Geoffrey thinking aloud. And while its thoughts arise from conditions in which the soldier was the chief figure, it is difficult to think that the book was intended for him. Some of the verse was, true enough; but *The Hardest Part* is in fact a theological book of a novel kind: and while it came out of the war, it outlasted the war. It was being reprinted seven years afterwards, and is quoted to this day.

Naturally, since the book represents Geoffrey's thinking, it has central to it the theme of God as one who suffers with mankind, rather than looks down 'a staring splendour, like the sun' in remote omnipotence. The very title comes from one of Geoffrey's dialect poems, *The Sorrows of God*.

> The sorrows of God must be 'ard to bear
> If 'e really 'as love in 'is 'eart.
> And the 'ardest part i' the world to play
> Must surely be God's part.

In his very early days as a padre, Geoffrey writes in his introduction, he went to see an officer in a base hospital. This would be at Rouen, about the time when he was frequenting the *Rive Gauche* canteen. The sick man, voicing thoughts which may well have been with him in long hours of lying in bed, asked his visitor what God was like. There was a crucifix over the bed. Geoffrey pointed to it. The result was not what he had expected. The young man found the sacred emblem puzzling and repulsive: puzzling because the victim figure seemed quite irreconcilable, when one really gave the matter a moment's thought, with the idea of God Almighty; repulsive because it was apparently held by Christians in some extraordinary way to represent a perfectly futile plan for saving the world from sin. And he went on to say that the plan, if such it could be called, appeared to be a thoroughly bad one because it hadn't worked. Anyone who supposed the world was in any sense free from sin had better take a trip to the front, not so far away, and see for himself. "I asked you," the young man concluded, "not what Jesus *was* like; but what God *is* like. To me he is still the unknown God."

It was a challenging beginning. Geoffrey went through at least two battle periods with the question burning in his mind, and the stark experiences which came his way made it burn all the more intensely. One thing was clear; the traditional presentation of Christianity had been weighed in the balance and found wanting when it came to reconciling what was taught about God, about prayer, about the sacraments, with the harsh facts of life as war revealed them. If God was omnipotent, why did he allow such horrors to exist. If prayer was the power it was said to be, how came it that it appeared to be so ineffective? What was the real meaning behind such phrases as 'the resurrection of the body' and 'eternal life'? Above all, what was the answer to the question posed from that Rouen hospital bed; what was God like as seen in the Bible, in history, in prayer, sacrament and the Church? Such questions were given urgency amid circumstances where prayer could be mistaken for cowardice, where death frequent and bloody, came suddenly upon the just and the unjust, and where the whole world seemed to be mad and bad. Geoffrey's purpose in *The Hardest Part* was, in Moore Ede's words to 'bring religion into relation to the stern realities of life, and free it from the deadening conventionalities of thought and practice'.

It was a bold undertaking, and the method was striking, even shocking at that time. "During active operations," Geoffrey wrote, "I was very busy and intensely preoccupied, unconscious of any connected thinking. Yet when a lull came I found in my memory whole trains of thought that had been working themselves out all the time. Each I have tried to write down as memory gave it to me."

Thus each of his trains of thought starts from the memory of a particular event and thereafter wanders wide. A sector of trench is caught in a heavy bombardment. It lasts two hours, during which it is possible only to cower down and keep still. In occasional pauses between the immense crashings and howlings a sergeant can be heard cursing vividly, and a man next to him praying aloud, despairing and shivering, for safety. The realisation comes to Geoffrey with some force that it is the praying which is by far the more disgusting, and the thought was made more disturbing by the realisation that a great deal of the prayer, in peace as in war, was in fact of that order, if not of that urgency. What, then, was prayer which was not contemptible, or selfish, or useless? His answer has long survived the passing of the conditions which posed the questions. True prayer, when it is of that kind which asks, is for courage to endure, never for permission to survive. It is not a protection against any calamity in any day or age. It will not preserve in that sense any more than it saved the Christ of Gethsemane from the imminent cross. But it will ensure that, whatever particular cup of bitterness has to be drunk, neither fear nor the consequences of it will destroy the essential self. Such a condensation does violence to the quality of Geoffrey's answer to the question posed for him by the two voices heard in the lulls between heavy shelling; the one cursing; the other praying to be spared. (Incidentally, the man of prayer was duly blown up.) The question abides, and always will, while human suffering endures.

And then again there was the corporal who, with others, attended Communion before one of the summer battles on the Somme in '16. Geoffrey noticed the splendour of his physique as he bent over him with the words: "Preserve thy body and soul unto everlasting life." Three days later, in one of his customary post-battle wanderings about, he found the same body, terribly mutilated, in a shell-hole. The incident is the starting point for a thinking aloud upon what the sacrament really means, as distinct from what it is often said to mean. Why did this boy make his Communion before the fight? Did he take 'preserve thy body' literally? Or was it thoughts of home? Or was it a kind of self-dedication, something it was felt 'ought to be done' before an important occasion? If it was any of these reasons which brought the boy to his last Communion, then the fault lay at the door of all the faulty teaching which has abounded for so long upon this vital matter. He proceeds, in a brilliant chapter, to outline some of the consequences of thinking of the great sacrament as something remote from life, reserved for the zealous few: 'Many old and middle-aged women, some young girls, and a few very respectable men.' And why was this so, why was it that the norm in so many churches was a tiny nucleus of such 'regular communicants' as they were called, surrounded by a much larger circle of the irregular, which was in its turn encompassed by a still wider circle of those not interested at all?

His answer is worth quoting: "I wonder if we have not made the Sacrament an end in itself rather than a means to an end, the great end of Christ-like life. It has seemed to the man in the street that we were trying to persuade him that regular and frequent attendance at this service would of itself avail to save his soul, and secure him entry into heaven hereafter. We have failed to connect the Sacrament with life . . . Of course, in theory we are just as much opposed to magic and mechanical religion as he is; but in practice we sail close to it . . . The Churches tend to become ends in themselves . . . We have been calling men to services when what they wanted was the call to service." And when to all this, he goes on, is added the complexity with which the doctrine of the Eucharist has been surrounded, and to that the bitter, age-long controversies which have divided Christians at this very point, can it be wondered at, he asks, that so many in the outer circles stay away altogether?

So much is destructive only, a manifestation of the critical spirit which the war had aroused in many of the best chaplains regarding what all had come to see as the inadequacies of the Church as they had known it. There were others, besides Geoffrey, feeling keenly that—'We have our small band of devotees; but the great tide of restless, vigorous life sweeps by our doors and finds outlet in a thousand other ways."

This critical spirit is reflected in the book *The Church in the Furnace*, a collection of essays by seventeen Anglican Chaplains serving in France and Flanders at that time. Four future bishops were among the contributors; Barry, Woodward, Kirk and Woods: so was a future Dean of York, Milner-White, and the novelist George A. Birmingham, alias Canon Hannay. Geoffrey is among them, and took vast trouble over his essay, on *The Religious Difficulties of the Private Soldier*. They were all very angry, full of the things which would have to be done in the promised time when war should be no more. Some of them have been done, too, so that Geoffrey's picture in the chapter on God and the Sacrament in *The Hardest Part*, of a pietistic inner core as the chief frequenters of the altar is no longer true. The growth of the Parish Communion has altered that to some considerable extent. Nor are the divisions between what he calls 'Church and Chapel' anything like as deep and bitter as in his day.

Many things, indeed, have altered—and for the better. The Church has been through another furnace since then, and is possibly, with many other institutions, now in sight of a third, this time having nuclear temperatures in which objects do not so much melt, to resume other shapes later, but vanish altogether. Meanwhile, however, one challenging truth remains still as regards the Church in this modern world: that past its doors "the great tide of restless, vigorous life sweeps by, and finds outlet in a thousand other ways".

But there was a constructive side to what Geoffrey here has to say in this book about the Sacrament which was so absolutely central to his own life. And this abides, speaking still, the very words throbbing with some of the passion which could make his voice so memorable: "The Sacrament . . . is the heart, the blood-centre, of the great army of people who, having seen and loved God in Christ, are resolved to fight for and suffer with him unto death and beyond it. It is the appointed means and method of meeting God. That bread is the ration of a fighting army. That wine is the stirrup-cup of a band of knights who ride out to an endless war—"

It is a personal testimony, a noble vision of what he felt ought to be, rather than an accurate picture of what is. Yet it is part of the function of a prophet to see visions and to dream dreams, and here he was doing both. And still his cry goes up; "God, turn the Church from an ambulance into an army, and make it really militant upon earth. Do we love God? Do we love the suffering God, and do we want to suffer with him? Do we find him in the Sacrament? Ritual does not matter; the manner of the Presence does not matter. They are not essentials. Nothing really matters but the love of God in Christ."

Such matters may seem to range far from the starting-point of the body of the corporal in the shell-hole. But the impression is a false one. That pathetic image looms behind the argument of the whole remarkable essay, like some blown-up photograph filling the back of the set in a television discussion. It is the same throughout the book; only the picture changes with the topic, and each picture is a period-piece. So the chapter on God in History begins with a 'still' of a captured German strong-point lit by a candle which keeps going out in the draught of concussions outside. The floor is covered with wounded. And the chapter on God and the Life Eternal has a horrid picture of Geoffrey's friend and batman, nineteen-years-old Roy Fergusson, leaning against a pile of sandbags, his head buried in his hands, a great hole in his back. And when the theme moves to God and the Church, behold, the picture changes yet again, this time to a big man, heavy jawed, deep lines round eyes and mouth, kneeling on the lip of a shell-hole, somewhere in the Ypres Salient in '17, still gripping his rifle. He had been shot neatly through the forehead. From his pay-book Geoffrey discovered his name —Peter. And immediately his thoughts go to another Peter, the big fisherman of Galilee, and how he was an 'average man', too. The difference between them was that the first Peter had had all the latent strength and goodness in him aroused. But no one, and certainly not the Church, seemed able to do much in that line for his modern namesake. Here in this chapter can be discovered the beginnings of that emotional self-identification with the 'ordinary man' which was the key to Geoffrey's thought and action in the post-war years.

And now those years were fast approaching. For Geoffrey, in spite of the fame which by then had gathered about him—war's end came, not with a bang, but a whimper. The man who disembarked at Folkestone on March 21st, 1919, was a very different person from the eager, ingenuous priest who had gone out at the Christmas of '15. Like the wedding-guest after his encounter with the Ancient Mariner, he was a sadder and a wiser man. Both words fit him exactly; the sadness which had always underlain his surface exuberance became henceforth more marked; and a deeper wisdom, that of a man who had learned much in a very dark valley of the shadow, added weight to the rest of the message which he had still to give.

Like so many of his generation, he returned to civilian life embittered, above all conscious of the many, the very many, who did not come back at all. Among these, a little group, were some of his own sort. Tubby Clayton of Toc H, mentioned some of these chaplains in aftertimes:

"Rupert Inglis, serving with my own Brigade, went out upon the Somme to bring men in, and brought some; then went out again and disappeared. Hardy, orphan son of a struggling commercial traveller, the greatest of them all. Dick Dugdale, transferred to win a hostile Colonel. He won him in a month; they died together." And then he added words which may serve as an epitaph, when all the critics have had their say, upon these padres of that old war. "They were true priests, true men. The Church scarce knew she held them. Their names are now forgotten; but many men's hands welcomed them into Paradise."[1]

Perhaps it might have been a happier end for Geoffrey if he had been among them. But there was work yet for him to do. Meanwhile, it fell to him to express, in tremendous and bitter lines, what so many came to feel about the monumental, historic anti-climax to the years of tragedy which came with the

[1] P. B. Clayton: *Fishers of Men.*

Treaty of Versailles. He called this cruel poem *Dead and Buried*—

> I was crucified in Cambrai
> And again outside Bapaume;
> I was scourged for miles along the Albert Road,
> I was driven, pierced and bleeding,
> With a million maggots feeding
> On the body that I carried as my load.
>
> Yet my heart was still unbroken,
> And my hope was still unquenched,
> Till I bore my cross to Paris through the crowd.
> Soldiers pierced me on the Aisne.
> But 'twas by the river Seine
> That the statesmen brake my legs and made my
>   shroud.
>
> There they wrapped my mangled body
> In fine linen of fair words,
> With the perfume of a sweetly scented lie,
> And they laid it in the tomb
> Of the golden-mirrored room,
> 'Mid the many-fountained garden of Versailles.

Some little while after the March of 1919 'an ugly little man, with wonderful eyes, wearing an immense collar', presented himself in the study of the vicarage of St. Martin in the Fields. The vicar looked at him with curiosity. It was the famous Woodbine Willie.

CHAPTER V

THE DEVELOPMENT OF WOODBINE WILLIE

WHAT first brought Geoffrey to St. Martin's H. R. L. Sheppard could not afterwards remember. What did stay in his mind was the impression his visitor made, and that in spite of a good deal of unfavourable report about Geoffrey which had already reached him. It had reached many people, and the shadow of disapproval never left Geoffrey to the end of his days. It might at this time have engulfed him altogether but for the understanding of the King in making him a royal chaplain. Sheppard knew of these things. He had suffered himself, and was to suffer more, from adverse criticism.

He found at that first meeting those mannerisms of which ill-report had spoken—language strange and strong, an apparent determination to make an impression at any price. But he found also something else, a sincerity so absolute as to redeem all.

As usual, Geoffrey began by speaking off the top of his head, continuing verbally the topic he happened to be thinking of. On this occasion it chanced to be the subject of Christ, so that Sheppard found himself listening with some astonishment to a monologue on the theme. There began then a friendship between these two which lasted until each in his turn passed from the scene, and which survived the irritation which from time to time the one caused in the other. Each meant much to his day and generation. F. R. Barry, Vicar of St. Mary's, Oxford, and later Bishop of Southwell, held that Studdert Kennedy, with Tubby Clayton (founder of Toc H) and Dick Sheppard were probably the only parsons of whom that celebrated character, the man in the street, in the twenties ever heard, or in whose opinions he showed the smallest interest.

It may well have been so. The early twenties were strange times; embittered, disillusioned, poisoned by a sense of anticlimax so absolute that the only possible answer, among thinking people, at any rate, seemed to be one of an all-pervading cynicism. "The extraordinary fact remains," wrote C. F. Masterman in 1922, "that in both the two great interpreting branches of literature, fiction and poetry, not only has the war given no real inspiration but, among the young, bitterness and contempt of the foolishness of men is far more noticeable than any new inspiration." The picture presented, he goes on to say, was usually of a contrast between a materialist pre-war society having given place, for a brief while, to the self-sacrificial temper of the war itself, only to be succeeded by a return to the former ills distinguished by an even more determined resolve, on the part of many, to grab the pleasures of the hour. This third stage was "one of complete disillusion and disgust. of hatred of the old men who have sent the young to die . . ."[1]

The Church came in for its full share of the blame which was held, however unjustly, to lie at the door of any established institution which had seemed to acquiesce in the death of a generation. It was a difficult time for religion. Two incidents which befell Geoffrey himself in the immediate post-war years had a dark significance in this context. The first was recalled long afterwards by Sheppard. Geoffrey was to preach in St. Martin's at a service for men and women in uniform. "It was a time," Sheppard recalled, "when the whole world seemed to be tottering, when anything might have happened, for many of those in uniform were tired of discipline, and angry—" And then this dangerous congregation saw in the pulpit "a strange little man, wearing a Military Cross on his surplice". He held them spellbound as he acknowledged in burning words the justice of their resentments and then passed on to show the futility of a barren rage. Many, Sheppard said, "had come to the Church almost insane; they left it perfectly cured . . . yet the

[1] C. F. G. Masterman: *England after War.* 1922.

lesson was taught with infinite sympathy, and with an obvious and passionate love for those who were passing through a difficult time."[1]

But then, Geoffrey was himself doing the same thing. There were those who met him in these years who judged him to be definitely off-balance, as were so many who came back from the war to find what was left almost intolerable. If others were bitter, so was he: if others had been sorely tried, so had he. And the pain was made all the more acute by the uncomfortable capacity, common to those of deep sensitivity, to identify himself with the sufferings of others. True, the agony did not now come from encounter with the physical brutalities of war so much as from the spiritual mass-casualties who staggered back into civilian life, as often as not to find themselves unwanted. "That chap *must* have been on the dole," one such unfortunate once said of Geoffrey, after hearing him speak, "or he could never talk like that." So similarly, in these immediate post-war years, there were many who felt likewise when they heard him speak. He *must* have been through it all himself. And that, of course, was true.

The second incident befell in, of all places, the London School of Economics, and came to light in a curious way. A woman who for forty years had sent, without explanation, an annual subscription to the offices of the Industrial Christian Fellowship with which Geoffrey came to be associated, was asked eventually why she did so. She replied that it was in token of long-remembered admiration for his courage and patience when, during her student days, he visited the School. She wrote:

"He received a hostile reception. The message of a Christian padre was not a welcome one, and I expect

[1] *G. A. Studdert Kennedy: By His Friends.*

116

the occasion was thought of as a chance to show Woodbine Willie a thing or two. The students were noisy from the start; stamping, throwing bread rolls, tomatoes, rolled-up newspapers. S.K., after trying to make himself heard, stood in silence, not moving. He was a small man, not of commanding presence. In the end he was heard. Afterwards, he seemed very exhausted.

"How did he impress one? He made an impact that could not be avoided. He seemed to know—really to know—that he had found what men sought, and must tell them of it. But he knew also that they would not listen and I think, like our Lord, wept over Jerusalem. Perhaps he knew his time was short. As he stood on that platform I felt, though I was not then a Christian, that we saw another Stephen, of the twentieth century. I never saw him again. But I never forgot him. I could still take you to the exact bus-stop in Regent's Park where I opened an *Evening Standard* and read of his death, which came as a personal shock."[1]

Both these events took place in what was for Geoffrey essentially a time of transition. At the end of the war he returned, as so many others returned, to the place he had left, at the close of 1915. In the March of 1919, three and a half years later in time, but an age away in experience, he was still Vicar of St. Paul's, Worcester. His work was there; his family was there, a family to be increased, in January 1921, by the birth of a second son, Christopher. Yet—also like many others—he was to find it difficult, indeed impossible, to resume a life that in truth, had changed radically. Or perhaps it would be more accurate to say that he had himself changed, or been changed, so fundamentally, that the framework of

[1] Private information.

life which had once fitted him well, was no longer large enough to contain him.

There were, in Geoffrey's case, at least three other reasons why any resumption of the old life was not really a tenable proposition. In the first place, he had become a national figure—his fame followed him around, and with it came the inevitable demands on him to speak here, there, everywhere. The press-cuttings of the period show him turning up in an odd variety of places: from St. Martin's to Buckingham Palace to preach before George V (who took care to hear him at least once a year henceforth). And of course all the time there were the invitations to be the *pièce de résistance* at provincial occasions. *Famous Army Chaplain's Visit to Wellingborough*, is the headline on one cutting representative of many. "The Vicar of St. Paul's, Worcester, known under the pseudonym of 'Woodbine Willie', visited the town on Sunday and spent a very busy day."

He did indeed. Geoffrey preached in the morning, inspected a parade in the Market Square afterwards; preached at a service for men in the afternoon; preached at evensong, upon which occasion "the church was crowded and the choir sang unaccompanied their prize selection; 'He that shall endure to the end'."

It was an appropriate choice. How long any man, especially one who lived on his nerves to the degree Geoffrey did, can endure that kind of thing, is an unsolved problem which remains still of great importance. It killed Geoffrey within ten years. It removed from a world which bitterly needed him one of the greatest of all Archbishops, William Temple, likewise at a sadly early age. The loss in both cases was tragic—and unnecessary. The words which F. A. Iremonger, Temple's biographer, used of his subject after the second world war could with equal truth have been said of Geoffrey after the first: "As I looked across the hearthrug at that spent man with the tired eyes and ill-regulated engagement-book whom Christians of every name were trusting for leadership and inspiration in the post-war years I could only ask, with shame and amazement; 'Is the Church so rich in prophets that it can afford to squander the gifts of God?'"[1]

Of course, it is often the prophet's own fault. Prophets are not good at saying 'no'. But it is a pity when no one at least tries to do it for them.

Geoffrey's need at this time—though he may well have been reluctant to acknowledge it—was for a platform, a secure base from which he could have gone out to carry his message and to which he could have returned to refresh himself as occasion offered. Some saw the need; representations were made at this time with regard to a possible canonry of Worcester. But it was not to be. And so yet another great man was allowed, no one hindering him, to start upon that fatal path of sick hurry and divided aims, somewhere along which there lurks in ambush the inevitable coronary or failing heart. No one wants a prophet to be comfortable, least of all the prophet himself. But nobody is any the more edified when he has to write his books in the train, flog himself to speak when the tired brain rebels, or listen to a thousand choirs giving their prize selections.

However, for Geoffrey the full impact of this kind of life had not yet arrived. He was still Vicar of St. Paul's, Worcester. Meanwhile, if his fame pressed upon him many extra burdens, so also did the ferment within himself. This was the second element which made any return to a pre-war pattern of life so diffi-

[1] F. A. Iremonger: *William Temple*. O. U. P.

cult. If he had become a national figure, he had also become a different man. The Chaplain of the *Rive Gauche* Canteen was dead. In place of that ingenuous participant in a just war there stood now an infinitely more mature person equally convinced that no war could be just.

This is not the place to examine Geoffrey's pacifism which, never being of the same emotional simplicity as Dick Sheppard's, did not have the same popular appeal. He had not as yet, in these years immediately following the war, sorted out his own mind on this, as on many other matters. But he was in process of doing so, and that is the significance of this period in Geoffrey's life. He was thinking his way through the huge barbed-wire entanglement of problems in which the war had left him. What is more, he did a good deal of his thinking aloud, and it was very brilliant and very helpful to many who in those times found themselves enmeshed in a similar situation. If, for instance, the whole of Western civilisation had been unable to prevent itself drifting into that vast corporate sin which the war had been, was it not necessary to probe deep into the causes, and to find what was wrong with a society in which such things could be?

Yet war was but one symptom of a general malaise of which poverty was another. The threadbare society which he had encountered in Leeds and Rugby and Worcester—indeed all his life with its background of slum parishes—now came up in his mind for much closer examination. Why was it necessary: what was the remedy? Was Socialism the answer? Was Marx the answer? Did there in fact gleam beyond the darkness which had come upon Russia in 1917 the possibility of a juster world order? Such questions, forty years on, may well look antique, like a car with bulb horn and gears outside. But they were pressing enough then, and were the origin of much of the Christian thinking on social and economic matters which characterised Geoffrey's message in the next decade. And since his was a profoundly Christian mind at work on them, the message itself does not date as do the events which drew it forth. And it may here and at once be said that it was seminal to a degree which has scarcely been recognised. Many, including William Temple himself, owed much to the passionately hard thinking which Geoffrey was doing in these years.

Naturally, when he thought aloud on such matters, he chose his audience. Certainly, to such gatherings like the one at Wellingborough he gave of his best, because he loved them so dearly. As was once said of him—"He and a crowd were made for each other". "He has a rich Irish brogue," noted one reporter, "and everyone much enjoyed the breezy utterances that fell from his lips." But it can scarcely have been breezy utterances which led to the inscription on a cigarette box still to be found in his widow's Worcester house: *To The Rev. G. A. Studdert Kennedy, M.C., In grateful remembrance of visits to the British Embassy Church, Paris, 1919.*

He could be so many things, to so many men. Perhaps that is partly why he has been so forgotten, since his effort was spread over so wide an area of understanding. How then shall we see him as he was in the early twenties? As good a picture as any, and as sound a judgment, came from James Adderley, in a press-cutting of the time, who encountered him in these years and indeed succeeded him as Rector of St. Edmunds, Lombard Street: "I have seen and heard most of the great preachers of the last thirty years. I have never seen anyone who created such enthusiasm, unless it was Father Ignatius. I have sat under

Father Maturin, Stanton and Dean Hole. I was an intimate friend of Dolling and Knox Little. None of them approached Kennedy. Continually one is hearing of fresh fields in which he is making a name. Very few parsons can take a retreat, thump a tub in the park, advise business and working men, write readable theology and passionate poetry, and be acceptable at Court, all at the same time. The only fear," he added prophetically, "is that he should do too much."

A third element which made resumption of pre-war life so difficult was that there was very little pre-war life to resume. Everything was different: even though outwardly things might appear the same. True enough, St. Paul's, Worcester, was still there, and the people went about the streets, and the Cathedral clock chimed the hours by the Severn which still flowed unalterably by the county cricket ground. But in fact it was a time of the breaking of nations; a time of discord, a time of the bursting forth, like prickly buds on a bare tree, of many discontents. "Those who tried to put the clock back found merely that it no longer told the time. The Edwardian epoch, which continued in essentials until the first world war, was found, when hostilities had ceased, to have receded into the background of history. It was as remote as the *ancien régime* after the Napoleonic wars."[1]

So some fame, and profound changes in himself, and equally, radical and bewildering ones in the whole pattern of contemporary life, made these years of return, 1919 to 1922, difficult for Geoffrey. All the time he was writing. Two books which came from him at this time, even by their titles alone, reflects the prevailing mood: *Lies* was one. *Food for the Fed Up* the other. A reporter on a Worcester paper, who met him in connection with the first of these books,

[1] James Laver: *Edwardian Promenade*. Hulton. 1958.

twenty years later from memory drew an admirable picture of Geoffrey as he must then have been.

"It was in his role as a writer that I first made contact with Studdert Kennedy. Overwhelmed with applications for articles and books, as well as travelling all over the country preaching and lecturing, he came to a friend who was editor of an evening newspaper in Worcester, asking him to recommend a stenographer. So he was sent into the reporters' room, where he sat himself on the back of a chair and told his errand. I was fascinated with the man and arranged to see him later.

"There followed many pleasurable evenings together —most of my duty-free time being spent at St. Paul's Vicarage. Studdert Kennedy was doing the series of articles which he subsequently published as *Lies*. He would dictate at tremendous speed, smoke and choke; then, if he had not made his meaning thoroughly clear, he would scrap it all and start again.

"In a very real sense it may be said that Studdert Kennedy helped to make Jesus Christ real to the ordinary man. At Worcester I often met him and his curate in the immediate post-war days at a midday meal in the Communal Kitchen. In the Christian Social Union in the city he was a leader, and he was sure to draw a big crowd as a speaker at the Worcester Brotherhood. This meeting was held on a Sunday afternoon in the Congregational Church. He loved the rostrum. There was room for him to walk up and down. He began by quite unconcernedly throwing his leg over the side and asking, 'You remember that bloke that came to Jesus by night?'"

It was another journalist—a kind of man for whom Geoffrey seemed to have particular attraction—who, tracking him down when Geoffrey was on holiday at Eastbourne in 1920, also left an interesting picture of him. "He is one of the most inspired talkers that you could meet. He has all the real conversational *flair*: the vivid phrase, the heaven-sent adjective, the fire of the controversialist: and then, suddenly, the rapt air of the mystic, of the communer with old forgotten, far-off things, and, swift as the turn of a kaleidoscope, the balanced pronouncements of someone who has really studied a subject and gone down to its roots."[1]

But it would be false to suggest there was any vestige of a success story about Geoffrey's life at this time. There never was at any time: his true life flowed too deeply for such surface phenomena to be of importance, and often the stream of it was dark and sombre. That suffering Christ of the broken body whose image had so haunted him in France was equally an ever-present reality in these times of peace. Suffering, ugliness, poverty and injustice he saw everywhere. Some maintained that he was unbalanced in this, also, as in other attitudes to life. So, in spite of the surface outward ebullience, he remained what he had always been, a sad man; full of doubts and difficulties, kept going only by the steady gleam of faith, like a light seen across darkness amid the benighted wilderness of life.

For wilderness it was—indeed, as it still is. Yet there would seem to have been an especially bitter quality, a kind of sourness in the air of those early twenties not known before. The impression received by the wanderer through the silent corridors of those times is a very strange one, as of an enormous, circumambient grief. A man of some psychic sensitivity, known to the writer of these words, even in the later thirties visiting at evening a military cemetery near Passchendaele, found himself so affected by the atmosphere of the place that he had hurriedly to leave

[1] *Eastbourne Gazette*. August 25th, 1920.

it. The cult of the war-dead which was such a feature of the twenties had no parallel after the second war, even though its outward forms may have been to some degree maintained in the form of custom. Too many men had died too recently to allow life to be comfortable for the living in the twenties. Too many memories fluttered like moths in the windows of too many private lives. Bereavement was everywhere. Tens of thousands of women in the prime of life who should have been bearing their children found themselves condemned to the secret, never to be discussed tortures of the unsatisfied, until the fires of desire burned out with time, and all that was left of a husband, maybe, was a photograph, a telegram and perhaps a pipe, still faintly redolent of masculinity, and bitten at the stem. And too many parents were left like the shy father, described in a terrible passage in A. L. Rowse's *A Cornish Childhood* who, having attended the unveiling of a memorial window in the local Grammar School, stopped an uncomprehending prefect to explain that his son's name had been wrongly spelt.

Such were some of the realities behind the cult of 'Lest we Forget'. The trouble was that the sorrow was so large-scale, and darkly suspected of having been unnecessarily incurred. As Geoffrey himself reflected in the verses *Dead and Buried* the prevailing bitterness, so also is the grief caught in:

Let me forget—let me forget,
I am weary of remembrance
And my brow is ever wet,
With tears of my remembrance,
With the tears and bloody sweat—
Let me forget.

But that was not so easy. The circumstances of the living also often gave little enough cause for cheer.

Too many had too obviously done well out of the war, and were looked upon with sullen anger by those who, it seemed, had lost their places in the rat-run of a competitive society by gallantly absenting themselves a while. So the unemployed old soldier, and the ex-officer with frayed cuffs, formed a sombre background to times out of joint. And always there were the disabled whose tragedy was lived out behind the closed doors of many a home to which a shattered man had been returned. Typically, in one of the dialect poems, *The Pensioner*, Geoffrey chose to show what this could mean in a humble household. The speaker is a working-class woman of the little streets landed, until death chose to part them, with a human wreck:

> I should be most 'umbly grateful
> And just do as best I can.
> But my pension won't buy kisses,
> An' 'e'll never kiss again.
> 'E ain't got no kissin' in 'im,
> Ain't got nothing now—but pain—

The blow dealt by all this grief and disillusionment to the basic concept of a beneficent God was, naturally enough, staggering. Geoffrey summed up the prevailing mood in his introduction to *Lies*. "This post-war world is black with lies—biting and buzzing round everything. There's a bad smell about; like the smell of the dead. It is the smell of dead souls—"

And at the same time, as regards the life of the Church, other factors were at work equally inimical. "Many of the social habits whose continuance was calculated to sustain religious conventions, even where personal fidelity was weak, were quite suddenly destroyed by the war. There was the sudden fluidity of the nation, invading every home, as men left for army life. Great numbers of women entered industry on a scale without precedent. The habitual became humdrum, and there were all the new pressures on leisure time and the traditionally quiet Sunday."[1]

But above all it was the prevailing atmosphere of indifference which was so spiritually deadly, and this was the atmosphere in which Geoffrey was to live and labour for the brief remainder of his life. "History already sees those inter-war years as the unnecessary and wasted years throughout all of which the open cracks in society and the writing on the wall were visible . . . The pre-war social trends continued un-abated, and after a few years of unsettled industrial activity, the deterioration, leading to the Great Depression, set in."[2]

Food for the Fed-up, the best of Geoffrey's books of this period, was a tremendous piece of sustained apologetic. The 'fed-up' he saw as those many who had continued into civilian life those soul-rotting atti-tudes towards all that they had once believed which the brutal futility of war had implanted in them. And his method is, as though a sullen audience of such were before him, to go through the Creed clause by clause, re-stating its ancient truths in modern terms, straining every nerve to show its relevance and its necessity, and clothing all in memorable language. More here than in his later books, Geoffrey wrote as he spoke, the headlong prose disguising the careful thought that had gone to the making of it. Thus, on whether any credal statement is merely a formal dogma: "The Creeds are no more complete statements of truth than a soldier's love letter was a complete statement of his love." His wife "slept on it, lived with it, found it life and love and laughter; sun, moon and

[1] E. R. Wickham: *Church and People in an Industrial City.* Lutterworth Press. 1957.
[2] ibid.

stars. That is what creeds are—ridiculous as expressions, but wonderful as symbols . . . Poetry does not say what it means: it hints at it. So do creeds—"

And so on. It is difficult to believe that he ever sat down and wrote this kind of thing. It is spoken word. One can almost see, as probably the Worcester journalist who acted as amanuensis did see, the excited gestures which went with it as Geoffrey paced the study, late at night in St. Paul's Vicarage, chain-smoking the while. "If our Creed is only a form, that may be our fault. You can bet on this—you don't really believe your Creed until you want to say it standing at spiritual attention with the roll of drums in your ears, the light of love dazzling your eyes, and all the music of a splendid world crashing out a prelude to its truth."

Such dramatisation may well have seemed unbalanced, had it not been accompanied by a ballasting weight of thought. But it was. *Food for the Fed-up*, in spite of its cheap-jack title, was and is, a closely argued case for the validity of Christian truth, written, not for the already convinced, not for the theologian, but for the man with no time for either.

Nor was that all. The book is notable for its encounters with most of those arch-enemies of faith—materialism, determinism, pessimism, cynicism—with which he was to be in frequent conflict, in print as on platform and street corner, for the rest of his life. In particular it is noticeable how his old adversary of pre-war days—the doctrine of sexual freedom as popularly held to be manifested in Freudian psychology, exercises him here.

"There is the solution," he says, echoing first the arguments of the opposite side—a habit which even the gentle Sheppard found particularly annoying— "if you could somehow choke the priest with his pale-faced Christ, in which he does not believe himself, you would be free to live according to the true creed, which is that man is an animal. Get rid of the King and his enchantments, and be content to abide without, among the cattle of the field."

Perhaps because he felt personally involved, or maybe because he was particularly well informed, he attacked this enemy with singular intensity.

"It is a ghastly thing for one who has studied and come to understand the powers of suggestion to contemplate the unnatural alliance which has been formed between the specialist in his study and the fool in every street to debauch the minds of the people with a flood of new sex teaching."

There is an echo of the poem in his collected verse, *The Psychologist*.

> He takes the saints to pieces
> And labels all their parts,
> He tabulates the secrets
> Of loyal loving hearts.
> His reasoning is perfect
> His proofs as plain as paint.
> He has but one small weakness,
> He cannot make a saint.

But the real value of *Food for the Fed-up*, like the true worth of the writer of it, lay at a deeper level, and the many to whom the book came as an invigorating tonic in a spiritually debilitated age received it well. It was Christian apologetic of a new kind, in its combination of raciness with wisdom and understanding. Not surprisingly, it was, and indeed continues to be, imitated; though rarely with success. As Sheppard said, imitations of Studdert Kennedy were usually disastrous. For as the man was unique, so was his style.

Nor did he always succeed himself. *Lies*, which came out a year or so before *Food for the Fed-up*, lacks its cogency, smacks more of the street corner stand, and therefore has less in it of abiding value. Significantly, the anthology of Geoffrey's writings, *The Best of Studdert Kennedy*, published in 1947, quoted extensively from *Food for the Fed-up* and not at all from *Lies*. The latter as a book has died; the other lives still, a testimony to the truth of the statement made by his publishers at the appearance of the Anthology: "This generation needs Studdert Kennedy. His is the teaching for the kind of world we live in, and for the kind of people we are."

Meanwhile, as was inevitable, Geoffrey found himself increasingly drawn into the larger life of the Church of his day; so that to retrace his paths therein is to come upon many signs of the men and movements which, at the time, appeared to loom large within it.

Thus *The St. Martin's Review*, for the June of 1923, printed the following notice: "The Sixth Anniversary of the Life and Liberty Movement will be held on Monday evening in the Queen's Hall, Langham Place. Among the speakers are the Bishop of St. Alban's, the Dean of Manchester, and the Rev. G. A. Studdert Kennedy."

This was the movement which, together with other shared concerns, brought Geoffrey into contact and indeed into friendship with two great though diverse personalities of his time, William Temple and Dick Sheppard. Both, in their reactions to him, reveal something of Geoffrey himself.

The story of 'Dick' has been told well and often. How this intensely lovable man, eventually ordained in a steam of emotion after many private hesitations, in twelve years throughout the war and into the mid-twenties at St. Martin in the Fields exercised an amazing ministry, is a narrative which belongs to the history of his day. Sheppard, in the naïvety and gallantry of his idealism, typified one kind of reaction to the stresses of his time. Supremely a man of sensibility, truly a lover of his fellows, he was born to be loved, to be hurt, to have his heart broken in the course of his sentimental journey through life. True, there were other chapters in that life besides St. Martin's: before it Oxford House, Bethnal Green; and Grosvenor Chapel: after it the arid splendours of St. Paul's and Canterbury. But St. Martin's was the core of it, and St. Martin's was where Geoffrey, for some six months after the war attached to Sheppard's staff, met him in his prime.

"He made the Church the most widely known in London; himself the best-known and most loved parson in England: hundreds and thousands of men, for whom religion had meant routine, boredom, mumbo-jumbo, found it was exciting, moving, helpful, alive . . .[1]

The words are so similar to those used so often of Geoffrey that it is almost possible to think they refer to the same man. And when the story of Dick at St. Martin's goes on to reveal the passionate love for the destitute, the lonely, the troubled; the brilliant unconventionalities, the startling enterprise, and the laughter which was always getting mixed up with the tears, the similarities between the two grow more startling still. And beyond and beneath the surface similarities there is always the fact, curious and strange, that each eventually had to drink a cup of suffering to the dregs.

In their own day they were often compared. Thus

[1] R. Ellis Roberts: *H. R. L. Sheppard.*

the *New Statesman*, in a mid-twenties review, quoting a then recent book on contemporary preachers:

"The boyish wistfulness of Dick Sheppard is always winsome; but his prescription of a sympathetic good nature for the ills of tortured humanity is hardly convincing. Mr. Studdert Kennedy definitely says as much; he evidently thinks that an unarmed man might as well offer a biscuit to a hungry lion in its native jungle. Mr. Kennedy is a passionate and indeed almost savage critic of society and current politics. He has a knack of versifying, and a gift of coining phrases which bite and sting and reveal.

"His God is rather formidable and ruthless . . .'all down the ages He has stung, whipped, called, wooed, driven, sometimes it would almost seem, tortured men into life; for the last enemy which shall be destroyed is sloth'."

Therein lay the essential difference between them. Sheppard was nearly all heart: Geoffrey, contrary to popular opinion, was, if not all head, at any rate a man in whom head usually had the last word. Of the two, his was by far the greater intellect—an intellect which Sheppard at times found disturbing.

"He is a Saint—a real Saint," he once wrote of Geoffrey; "I've never met a great orator before who wasn't pleased with himself, only sometimes I wish he hadn't got quite so big a brain that causes him to worry over problems until they become positively insoluble . . . The result of Studdert on me is to send me away thanking God for him; but trying to think as he thought and tending towards despair at the immensibility of all that he has put before me."

And again, when Geoffrey's novel *I Pronounce Them* appeared; "Please tell me what you think of Studdert Kennedy's novel. I just can't read another word of him. I don't know why, and it's not jealousy."

Indeed it was not. No one wrote more movingly of Geoffrey at his death than Dick. Yet the mind dwells with curiosity upon this antipathy which at times momentarily overshadowed the loving relationship of two great Christian men. The world of Dick Sheppard, of the Peace Pledge Union, of good intentions overthrown by the hard-faced without too much difficulty, has vanished away long ago. The dictators went through its emotional idealisms like tanks through a hoarding bearing the legend, once the slogan of Sheppard and his many supporters, "War—We Say No." As Nurse Cavell discovered that patriotism was not enough, so perhaps it may be said of them that theirs was the sad discovery that emotion was not enough, either.

"Year by year," Sheppard wrote, "I grew to know Studdert better and to love him more deeply, for we often met and had hours of talk. We did not always agree; but we knew each other's ways."

And from that knowledge of Geoffrey, Sheppard drew a sketch of him which lives still: "As a companion Studdert was a sheer delight. His laughter was a thing of joy, and his smile had a never-to-be-forgotten radiance. He would sit in an armchair, smoking endless cigarettes and drinking countless cups of tea, while he thrilled us with his wisdom and humour. To go to a theatre with him was to have your attention removed from the stage to the companion by your side, who was laughing with enjoyment. Then suddenly, at a touch of pathos in the play, those wonderful eyes would grow large and sad, and he was not ashamed of letting tears fall down his cheeks—"[1]

The association between Geoffrey and William Temple was of another order, being necessarily that of the lesser with the greater. Few, if any men of his

[1] G. A. Studdert Kennedy: By His Friends.

day, and certainly not Geoffrey, can survive comparison with that tremendous figure without being revealed as of smaller stature altogether. Acclaimed by some as the greatest Archbishop since Augustine, Temple stood, and indeed stands yet, alone. Those who watched his bulky coffin being borne down the nave of Canterbury Cathedral on a November day of 1944, when even the heavens seemed to weep, were surely right in feeling that there was passing from their midst a man of a calibre not likely to be seen again for many a long day. To have enjoyed the love, respect and admiration of such an one is a testimony in itself to notable qualities, and Geoffrey from Temple had all three.

The two first met in incompromising circumstances. Temple, as Sheppard had been, found himself prejudiced against Geoffrey before personally encountering him, expecting to find one who affected extravagance of language as a deliberate means of calling attention to himself. But at the first meeting, in the house of the Headmaster of the King's School in Worcester, he received a different impression. Instead of the expected poseur he found a man so un-selfconscious as to be able to speak and act without any consideration of his own appearance, one way or the other. Geoffrey on that evening of the early twenties arrived late, talked for twenty minutes at high speed, then fell silent and remained so. The Temples observed him with curiosity and surprise. But it was not long before both, to use Temple's own words, "were under his spell".

Thereafter, for almost a decade, they were in frequent association. Any friend of a great, many-sided man has to accept the limitation of knowing him only on one or two of the many sides, and that would certainly have seemed to be so in the case of Geoffrey with Temple. Chiefly he met him in the area of concerns where the Christian as such looked at contemporary society, acknowledged his responsibility for it, and considered how best he may help to redeem it.

From the first, then, Temple recognised Geoffrey's quality. "Soon after the end of the war," he wrote, "men knew that there was among us a prophet of social righteousness in the true succession of Henry Scott Holland."[1] Such a testimony from such a man was remarkable enough in itself. And it is clear also that Temple was deeply struck on the one hand by Geoffrey's intellectual capacity, and on the other by the wholly unusual degree to which this was balanced by a profound sense of the divine compassion. Sympathy for individuals, Temple saw, was at the centre of Geoffrey's life, even though social and economic problems of man in the mass exercised his mind. Thus the numbers of people in all varieties of need — material and spiritual — the hard-up as well as the lonely or the lost, continued to seek him out.

There are some odd stories from these years. There was for instance, the woman who came to the Headquarters of the Industrial Christian Fellowship, and who, being asked to leave her name, said she was Queen of the Tarts. There was the representative of the Rationalist Society who, at an I.C.F. debate arranged to bring opposites into confrontation, rather clearly had the best of Geoffrey. A little later, seen at one of Geoffrey's meetings, and asked why, he said, "I'd go anywhere to hear him." And then again there was the woman, embittered to the point of violence by the loss of a husband, who was changed totally after an hour of talk with Geoffrey.

Temple judged him to be, in this capacity to carry

[1] ibid.

135

others on the heart, as he put it, the finest priest he had ever seen. Even so, it was a testing combination, this one of demagogery with a genius for personal counsel. At times, to some, it could be off-putting. A woman who came later to serve him with devotion in the I.C.F., at first encountering him at a Life and Liberty meeting, found him in every way excessive. It was difficult to believe, she found, that the retreat conductor she heard a day or so later reading from his Greek Testament, and then expounding so helpfully, so quietly, could really be the same man. "Don't forget," Geoffrey himself used to say, "the gift of eloquence is the most dangerous a man can be given." Certainly, he knew he possessed it; but the effects of the power he had continued to puzzle him to the end. As the years went by, and he became increasingly able to draw crowds he would say to himself often, as he entered a pulpit or mounted a rostrum to see an ocean of faces beneath "Lord, I can't understand it."[1]

Thus, then, in the early twenties, was the man who so profoundly affected Temple. How far his outlook affected the future Archbishop's is a question which becomes all the more interesting when certain passages in Temple's writings are compared with Geoffrey's. Thus Temple on Humility in *Christ in His Church*: "Humility means that you think of yourself, as a distinct person, out of count, and give your whole mind and thought to the object to which they are directed, to God Himself . . ." Geoffrey, on the same subject, in a broadcast address from St. Martin's, has this; "Humility means, not thinking little of yourself, but ceasing to think of yourself at all, becoming swallowed up in the great job and the great work which God has set you to do . . ."[2] The resemblance

[1] Private information.
[2] Quoted in *St. Martin's Review*, January 1925.

136

is striking, and similar instances, as in the case of
Geoffrey's teaching on the Eucharist in the pamphlet 'Bread' with Temple's own doctrine on the same
matter, can be found elsewhere. Between Temple and
Geoffrey there does seem to have been, in fact, a
cross-fertilisation of ideas in which, for once, the
former was not altogether predominant. Temple's
name will be remembered long among those of the
illustrious; honoured as that of one who, amid many
other concerns, gave leadership to that cause of
social justice which looked back to Christian Socialism
for its beginnings. It may likewise, perhaps, be included among the honours of the quaint Irishman who
was his friend for a while, and whose name is not
among those of the illustrious, that now and then, at
least, he stimulated the mind and warmed the heart
of so great a man.

Geoffrey resigned the living of St. Paul's, Worcester,
in 1922. It was high-time. He had by then far more
than a year been living the kind of public life, already deeply involved with the work of the Industrial Christian Fellowship, which made it impossible
to continue in such a position. The press-cuttings of
the time show him all over the place : now preaching
in York Minster in the February of 1921, "the finest
exposition of economics to which we had ever listened" in the opinion of one reporter : now involved
in a public dispute of some moment with, rather surprisingly, Ernest Bevin.

These two events are connected, and the connection is important to the story of Geoffrey's final years.
In York Minster, on February 21st, he had said; "The
service of humanity, the dignity and priesthood of
work, are the ideals which alone can heal the in-
terminable wranglings of Capital and Labour." A few

days later, in the Queen's Hall, London, he turned suddenly on 'the docker's Q.C.' formidably sharing the platform with Lang, Archbishop of York, Temple, Bishop of Manchester, and other notables of the day. Bevin had been urging, with the emotion which it is always safe to impart into a statement which commits one to nothing, 'that the Church should join hands with Labour, and together march against the curse of war'. This was too much for Geoffrey. He accused Mr. Bevin of attempting to reduce a complex question to a simple issue in order that they may fight on it, going on roundly to declare that the Labour Party was shirking thinking. They were bold words at the time, for anyone with any interest in mass acclaim. Even so, he was to suffer much, from those, more numerous then than now, to whom left-wing associations smacked of anti-Christ. Geoffrey was dead nine years after this collision with Bevin. The day following his death, his old chief, P. T. R. Kirk of the Industrial Christian Fellowship, went to the Dean of Westminster with the proposal that Geoffrey should be buried in the Abbey. "What!" was the reply, "Studdert Kennedy? He was a Socialist!" And since equally there were those who held that not to be left-wing smacked of anti-Christ, it may fairly be held that Geoffrey, together with Temple, for that matter, fell neatly between the two.

Somewhere among the press-cuttings of the early twenties is an account of a sad little ceremony at St. Paul's, Worcester, at which Geoffrey shed some of his tears, received a presentation, sang *The Mountains of Mourne*, while his wife played the piano, and made a speech. It was his farewell to Worcester. Two events had made this possible; his appointment to the living of St. Edmund's, Lombard Street, and his acceptance of the post of chief missioner for the Industrial Christian Fellowship. He was about to begin the last lap of his journey, and enter upon a new scene.

CHAPTER VI

THE MAN IN THE TRAIN

WHAT that scene was in its wider implications may be illustrated by certain events which took place towards the close of the gloomy year of 1926. The General Strike was months over. The much more prolonged Coal Strike had miserably faded away. At this juncture there appeared a press article by the Dean of St. Paul's, under the heading 'Interfering Parsons'. There was nothing surprising, of course, in yet another piece of journalism from Inge, that pillar of the Church who, as someone unkindly remarked, had become two columns in the *Evening Standard*. The Joad of his day, 'in divine and secular wisdom alike one of the principal public oracles for the last twenty years or more', according to *The Times* on his retirement, was usually writing about something. It might have been 'Sex Ignorance among the Clergy' or 'The Revised Prayer Book'. Most things were grist to Inge's peculiar and highly profitable mill. In this instance, however, his target was those clergymen—and they had been numerous and distinguished—who had intervened to try to effect a settlement of a dispute which had been as ruinous to the country as poisonous in its social consequences.

The sombre facts were these: trouble in the coal industry had been accumulating ever since 1918. A national strike in the following year was postponed by the appointment of a Royal Commission, whose recommendations were on the whole ignored. Two years later, de-control of the industry shattered its wage-structure. Upon the coalfields, in fact, had fallen already the economic blizzard which was to moan so dismally about the industrial scene for years to come, building up great drifts of bitterness and disillusion. There was plenty of both now, among the still pit-heads from Rhondda to the Tees. Meanwhile, yet another Commission was appointed. This, in the *Samuel Report*, published its findings early in 1926. Almost coincidentally with its rejection by the miners, the Government decided to discontinue its subsidy to the industry. And at that stark point, the Trades Unions, led by J. H. Thomas, decided to add their weight to the miners in their struggle. The General Strike, the most formidable industrial dispute Britain has known, opened at midnight of May 3rd, 1926. How and why it collapsed nine tense days later, on May 12th, belongs to the history of the twenties. Here it may be noted only that henceforth the miners were left to fight on alone—a fight which ended with virtual capitulation on November 20th of the same year. The Dean's strictures of 'interfering parsons' appeared shortly afterwards.

He was correct in his main contention, that there had been parsons, and that they had been intervening, if not interfering on this economic 'darkling plain'. The debatable point arose from his second contention, that they would have been better employed minding their own business. And since that question lay at the heart of the work which engaged Geoffrey for the rest of his life, it is relevant to look into the matter in some detail.

There had been clerical interventions on two occasions in the prolonged struggles arising from the coal strike. The first had begun with the initiative of a man by that time Geoffrey's chief, P. T. R. Kirk, General

Director of the Industrial Christian Fellowship. He it was who had been active in forming a group pledged to endeavour to bring together the contending parties. Davidson of Canterbury gave active support, and the General Strike itself gave urgency to the matter. Thirty-nine Bishops and all the Free Church leaders were signatories of a call to prayer broadcast from Savoy Hill when the country was already, to its profound astonishment, preparing for siege conditions. By May 7th, this group of Churchmen had been in contact with the Prime Minister and Ramsay Macdonald, both of whom had welcomed a further appeal for the withdrawal of the strike which the Archbishop was to broadcast on the night of May 7th. This time permission was refused.

Even so, the appeal was printed in an attenuated *Times*. It created much excitement, not only on account of its contents, with their three-point basis for a settlement; not only because it had been suppressed —Churchill had refused it also for the official *British Gazette*—but especially by virtue of its origin. Here was the Church interfering in a noticeable manner; here was the Christian voice being heard in economic and political affairs on a scale not equalled since the personal efforts of Westcott of Durham had made possible settlement of the coal strike of 1892. What is more, the intervention was apparently welcomed in those frightening May days. At any rate the T.U.C. sent a delegation to Lambeth to thank the Archbishop, and the Prime Minister expressed gratitude shortly afterwards. Later on, however, he did inquire in the House "how the Bishops would like it if he referred to the Iron and Steel Federation the revision of the Athanasian Creed".[1]

But it had been a notable effort. The second, on the

[1] William Temple: *Christianity and the Social Order.*

part of the same group, brought together Owners and Miners in a series of metings, mostly at the headquarters of the Industrial Christian Fellowship, appropriately enough, in those warring times, located in the Sanctuary, Westminster. It would be too much to say that they were successful. Seebohm Rountree, indeed, the Critical Quaker of York, who was also involved in efforts at reconciliation, claimed that the Church's intervention delayed settlement for many months. But the Church as such had been in the battle. That was the great thing. Some approved. Temple's biographer summed up one reaction thus:

"One result at least had been achieved by the Churches' group. Coming immediately as it did after the Archbishop's action in the General Strike, its intervention changed completely the miners' attitude to the Churches. By organised labour organised religion had hitherto been held to embody the reactionary spirit of a privileged caste."[1]

But some reactions were very different. Inge's, in his article, was very different. The 'interfering parsons', Inge maintained, were "obvious time-servers—a new type of parson, sprung from the ranks and soured by poverty and thwarted ambition who, finding their people bored with religion, and perhaps not having much to say on that subject themselves, gladly escape to politics, in which they see so much more excitement and actuality." Above all, if illogically for the purposes of his argument, they were "incorrigible sentimentalists who refused to look economic facts in the face".

Here was the heart of the matter. The main implication was that if they did look economic facts in the face they would be confounded by them. And behind that lay another, echoed in much correspondence of the time, that they had no business to do so

[1] F. A. Iremonger: *William Temple.*

142

in any event. How true was either? As to the first, the supposedly inexorable nature of economic law was a doctrine which, in a multitude of applications had made possible, as the whole process of industrialisation intensified, some of the horrors which were the price of it. Such degradations as Engels noted years later in Manchester and as Hook found in his parish in Leeds, were consequences of it. The saddest of these was that the shape of society which emerged from the process seemed to many fundamentally unchristian. But how could it be otherwise if, as was so generally assumed, the economy was subject to iron laws of supply and demand which could no more be deflected from their operation than the stroke of a piston could be made to go any other way from that for which it was built? And if people at times got caught in the machinery, that was unfortunate: but to blame the machinery was unrealistic. In fact it was more: it was subversive if done in the name of any political theory; it was at best sentimentality if done in the name of Christ.

Such views, sincerely held by generations even of the devout, made possible simultaneously two things: the acceptance of poverty in some parts of the economy as inevitable, like rain: and the deep suspicion by those most usually subject to it, of any religion which could acquiesce in such a view. The desperate man who, in a moment of bitterness, tore up Bible and Prayer Book in a slum of Hook's Leeds as the bells were ringing to church, was the forerunner of many who, like the miners before the Coal Strike of 1926, regarded organised religion as embodying the reactionary spirit of a privileged class. So the first implication in Inge's article—that it was vain to argue with economic laws, whatever their consequences to human nature—had a long history.

So had the second, that the economic and political field of human affairs was no place for specifically Christian intervention. "Seek ye first the Kingdom of God and His righteousness, and all these things will be added unto you" Inge had quoted, to which the *New Statesman* had rather well replied that it would be equally irrelevant to offer such counsel to a hungry child as to the industrially dispossessed. It was simply not true, as a writer in the *Methodist Recorder* about this time, in the course of this same controversy, pointed out, that the Church could admit any field of human interest and activity as beyond the frontier. It took cognisance of art and science; why not then also of economics and of working conditions? The same point had been made more succinctly by Henry Scott Holland years before: "The more you are interested in the Incarnation, the more you must be concerned about drains," or again by Bishop Weston of Zanzibar in 1923 at the Anglo-Catholic Congress: "It is folly, it is madness to suppose that you can worship Jesus in the sacrament when you are sweating him in the bodies and souls of his children."

But such voices were by no means the first to be raised on this issue. Nor is Inge's petulant outburst to be seen as more than a very minor footnote to the massive and complex theme of the re-discovery by the Church of its social responsibilities. Even so, it represents an attitude of mind by no means yet defunct. A cartoon of Low, published in the *Evening Standard* as late as 1943, and reproduced in Iremonger's *Life of Temple* shows the Archbishop being rebuked for concern in such matters. "Be warned sinner, turn to higher things," is the caption under one, showing Temple venturing to tamper with a golden calf labelled 'Sacred Tradition of Economics'.

It was Geoffrey's destiny to spend the last decade

of his life among similar concerns. And to see what he was doing there, it is necessary also to find out who they were who had been there before him. A way into all these questions is to be found through some understanding of the origins and objects of that body which henceforth claimed him—the Industrial Christian Fellowship.

The origins of I.C.F. were varied. It was a body which, if called upon to look to the pit whence it was digged, would have to lay claim to several fairly small excavations, like little lead mines on a moor, which had been made in the nineteenth century here and there on the industrial wastelands. The purpose of these workings had varied; some had sought an ultimate Christian law or sanction by which society ought, ideally, to be powered. Others had sought for ways of bringing practical Christian concern to the task of binding up some of the many sores of industrialism.

So here and there in those dark and smoky years of early Victorian England were some, at any rate, who felt the weight of Christian responsibility for the ills of society. That, on the whole, such persons figure comparatively modestly in the story of their times is indicative of the unglamorous nature of their concern, of its lack of precise definition as to aim and of the suspicion with which the whole enterprise was generally regarded. Exactly the same three difficulties attended the work of the I.C.F. in Geoffrey's day. The emergence of Christian Socialism, which had, as its chief adversary, indifference merging often into hostility, alike from the official Church as from the very working classes whose cause it sought to champion, exhibits all these characteristics which again can be found reflected in the I.C.F. story seventy years later.

Christian Socialism emerged after the failure of the Chartist Movement in 1848. Its founder, John Malcolm Fowler Ludlow, a member of the bar at Lincoln's Inn had in Paris witnessed the revolution of that year. Out of that experience was born in him the conviction that Socialism, as a new political portent, needed to be Christianised, needed a spiritual and moral basis. The sharing of this conviction with another remarkable man, F. D. Maurice, who had been equally stirred by the events of the year of revolutions, led, in association with Kingsley, to the birth of the movement. Intellectually, Maurice was the dominant figure. Kingsley for a time, under the pseudonym 'Parson Lot', was the movement's propagandist. A man of immense learning, the son of a Unitarian minister, ordained after many a doubt, Maurice was chaplain of Lincoln's Inn when, on an evening of 1846, the barrister Ludlow called upon him. The immediate purpose of the call was to ask the Chaplain's advice upon a project for "bringing to bear the leisure and good feeling of the Inns of Court upon the destitution and vice of the neighbourhood".[1] Little came of this initial approach: the barrister found the chaplain, a shy theologian, much withdrawn into his own affairs. Even so, a beginning had been made. And though the subsequent development of Christian Socialism as a movement was not propitious, its long term effects were considerable. The paper of the movement, *Politics for the People*, suffered the double indignity of arousing opposition and failing through lack of support. The evening classes which developed into the Working Men's College established in Great Ormond Street in 1854, had to struggle hard. The 'Society of Promoters', with its co-operative workshops, did not flourish. It was all, in any event, a very small enter-

[1] M. B. Reckitt: *Maurice to Temple.*

prise, a modest little mine in the industrial wasteland in which Victorian England laboured feverishly to grow richer. It was the thinking behind the movement rather than its attemps at practical expression of its ideas, which was to prove seminal as time went by.

Such then, was one of the pits from which the Industrial Christian Fellowship of Geoffrey's day, as of the present, had part of its origin. Its actual birth just after the first world war, when Geoffrey had returned to Worcester, arose from the fusion of two of the many societies which the emergence of a Christian social conscience in the nineteenth century had encouraged; the Christian Social Union and the Navvy's Mission. The Christian Social Union, founded by Henry Scott Holland and Charles Gore in 1889 had as its forerunner a body started in 1877 amid the slums of Bethnal Green by the Rector of St. Matthew's, Stewart Headlam, the supposed original of the Reverend James Mavor Morell in Shaw's *Candida*, "a Christian Socialist Clergyman of the Church of England, and an active member of the Guild of St. Matthew". There in the play he may still be met, accurately observed, vigorous and enthusiastic, with Maurice's *Theological Essays* on his bookshelves, a complete set of Browning, and Marx's *Capital*. The Guild had as its special object "to get rid, by every possible means, of the existing prejudices, especially on the part of Secularists, against the Church, her sacraments and doctrines, and to endeavour 'to justify God to the people' ". The last phrase, a quotation from Kingsley, indicated the ancestry of the union. The endeavour, expressed often in protests at social injustice, could at times take dramatic form, as when Headlam led the funeral procession of a workman, ridden down by a police horse during a Socialist demonstration, from Bow Street to Whitechapel Cemetery via the Strand. But the Guild was a small, esoteric affair, never very influential. Its importance, as was so often the case with these pioneer efforts, lay in subsequent developments to which in some measure it gave rise.

The Christian Social Union, a body of a different order and dimension, included among its founders some of the contributors to *Lux Mundi*. Its nature may be seen in its three objectives; to claim for the Christian Law the ultimate authority to rule social practice, to study how to apply the moral truths and principles of Christianity to social and economic problems, and to present Christ in practical life as living Master and King. The objectives thus laid upon its members the twin obligations of study and action.

So research amid such apparently unrewarding fields as *Charitable Agencies and Industrial Relief*, and *Housing and Town Planning*—two among the many subjects selected for study by the Christian Social Union in its Edwardian heyday—were in fact of the essence of the matter. Even so, emotion does sometimes break through—

> Judge eternal, throned in splendour,
> Lord of lords, and King of Kings,
> With thy living fire of judgment
> Purge this realm of bitter things—

The writer was that Henry Scott Holland, sometime Regius Professor of Divinity at Oxford, co-founder with Gore of the Christian Social Union.

Here, then, was one of the bodies from which the Industrial Christian Fellowship derived. The other, the Navvy Mission Society, was again of an entirely different nature.

Here was the social conscience expressed principally in action, but within a specialised area of concern. Navvy's, 'navigation men' were the pick and shovel diggers of early nineteenth century canals. The name stuck to any engaged in a labouring capacity upon public works. The years saw armies of them come and go. They built docks and reservoirs; the railway age brought them out in force. And to meditate before some such work today, and to note the magnitude of the labour this curve of embankment, that cutting, must have involved long before the days of earth-moving machinery, is to be moved to spare at least a passing thought as to who they were who sweated there. Where did they live? Who cared for their families?

The Navvy Mission, begun in 1877 by Mrs. Charles Garnett, was very interested in these questions; to which the answers were usually hard ones. Navvys were casual labourers; they lived where they could, and what happened when they or their families fell ill was nobody's business. They were outcasts. "Living in their own temporary villages, separated from the ordinary influences of a town or rural population," the first annual report of the society stated, "they consider themselves to be in a sort of Edomite relation to all around them, their hand against every man, and every man's hand against them."

The Mission moved in on this situation with four objectives. The first, expressed in the customary phrase of the time, was to promote the spiritual welfare of the navvys, which being translated, usually meant simply showing them that someone cared. The other three: to gather information as to the real living and working conditions, to make known to the hitherto uncaring Christian the true facts, and to promote practical help, together represented those elements of research and action characteristic of this kind of endeavour.

The Navvy Mission became a sizable affair in its

day. In view of the importance of the lay-missioner, the resident man on the spot, to the Industrial Christian Fellowship of Geoffrey's time, it is interesting to find this early enterprise working in the same way. There were thirty-nine of them by 1890, in mission rooms built on most big public-works sites.

Some crossed the seas. In Canada, as members of the Church Camp Mission, they followed the building of the Pacific Railway, in Australia of the Trans-Continental. In the first world war the Mission had a concern with the labour-battalions in France. It had quite a story, for the most part unknown. It vanished as the navvy vanished, with the passing of time. The embankment, the tunnel, the reservoir, the dock and the canal, are the navvy's memorial—and the Mission's. In 1919 it was incorporated into the Industrial Christian Fellowship. The Christian Social Union followed in 1920, and this story moves nearer to the point at which Geoffrey became chief missioner of the new society.

Its architect was, like Geoffrey himself, an Irishman, P. T. R. Kirk. Before the war, vicar of a large London parish, during it a chaplain, Kirk returned from it, as did many others of his generation, deeply concerned at the degree to which the Church was out of touch with a large part of contemporary society. Especially was it failing to get across, to any significant degree, to the great working masses who, the war having brought them together and revealed their hearts and minds, were plainly to be seen as separated by enormous gulfs of misunderstanding from anything the Church had to say. Such a concern was not peculiar to Kirk: it exercised many. The symposium *The Church in the Furnace*, published by a number of Army Chaplains during the war—Geoffrey was working on his own contribution to it while at Flixecourt in 1917—had been full of it. But Kirk's particular concern was the failure of the Church to bear witness to the lordship of Christ—the phrase echoes the language of the Christian Social Union—in industry, in the daily working life of men and women. And since the parochial organisation of the Church was unsuited to this task the Fellowship was formed, as a body of men and women sharing the same sense of need, to break through with the Gospel into the industrial hinterland. It stood for Christ as the living Lord and Saviour in every department of human life: it proclaimed the Gospel of redemption and renewal both for the individual and for society: it held this world, in spite of impressive evidences to the contrary, to be God's, and human sin to be the continuing causes of the separation of that world from the divine order.

The organisation brought into being to give effect to these aims was extensive, working outwards through Council and Executive Committee. It had a headquarters staff—people destined to acquire unforgettable memories of Geoffrey as time went by. It had Clerical Area Directors, charged with the task of organising the work of the Fellowship, especially of bringing home to church people their obligations as Christians, for the social order in which they lived—rarely an easy task, nor always successfully accomplished. And, basic to the whole enterprise, it had its lay-missioners, drawn from the ranks of industry, specially trained and then sent to bear their witness for Christ in factory, on street corner, and wherever they could find those to listen to them. This was hard and unglamorous work, to which some gave the best years of their lives. "In 1921 I was a miner," one of them recalled years afterwards, "1926 came along. By this time I was a trade union official. However, for some years I had been a lay-reader. I believed in social security, but I was also convinced we must have a new world order. If we were going to solve the problem of industry, we wanted something more. We wanted social righteousness. I became an I.C.F. Missioner . . . The work is hard; the life strenuous. We are missioners without glamour."

That was always true. Perhaps it was always true of the whole movement. One searches in vain for an end-product, some clearly definable object, by the attainment of which, or by the failure to attain it, the success of otherwise of the whole enterprise can be measured. And here one comes upon a haunting similarity with Geoffrey's own life, to which the customary criteria of success cannot be applied. It was a self-giving, a proclamation of great truths, a stirring of many hearts, and an opening at least of some eyes, with no earthly reward and little honour at the end of it. So the work of the Fellowship might perhaps be said to have been the creation of an atmosphere of Christian concern, involving the education, on the one hand of the Church, and on the other of the outsider, of their joint responsibilities. None of it makes sense unless the continuing background of it all is borne in mind; the indifference of the many, both Christian and non-Christian, the manifest evils of the social system, and the constant effort to proclaim, amid all this, Christ as the Lord of all Life.

To do that is never easy. But it was quite exceptionally difficult in the decade after the 1914–18 war, for these very reasons. Those who complain of the amount of stony ground upon which, in these later times, the word of God is likely to fall, might usefully reflect that there was a good deal more of it, and that it was considerably stonier, forty years ago. This was the situation which the Industrial Christian Fellowship had to face from the beginning. Its business was specifically with that stony ground, and therefore it was perhaps scarcely to be expected that any immediately spectacular fruit should grow there from its efforts. But this is the story of a man, not of a movement, and now is the time to see where Geoffrey fitted into the whole picture.

Few less propitious nor more challenging times for the creation of such a body as the Industrial Christian Fellowship could have been chosen than the early twenties. A long winter of industrial discontent was about to begin. The bad years, the wasted years, lay ahead, the age of the gathering storm internationally, and the queues ever lengthening at the ironically named Labour Exchanges, of folly and sourness and defeat when so much went wrong, and so little went right. Above all else, at such a time, the movement needed a prophet. Kirk found him in Geoffrey. How he found him he has himself revealed.

"It was my privilege, under the hand of God, to offer him the work which occupied the last years of his life. The Industrial Christian Fellowship . . . was preparing for a wider embassy of goodwill among the trades and industries of our land. We were in need of a Messenger. After hearing Geoffrey speak I had no doubt that his was the voice, and his the message, for which we were waiting. A long conversation, some correspondence, and he had accepted the call."[1]

Another major change in his life at this time made it possible for Geoffrey to give his whole energies to that work—the appointment to the living of St. Edmund's, Lombard Street. Henceforth, since his family remained in Worcester—a family increased in the March of 1926 by the birth of a third son, Michael —he was to have in effect three homes: Worcester

[1] G. A. Studdert Kennedy: By His Friends.

sometimes, St. Edmund's at week-ends, and the train often, the train taking a usually tired, frequently exhausted man to yet another challenge to all that he had to give. We must try to see him in all three if we are to see a little of him as he was.

Once, at the conclusion of a particularly exhausting campaign in the North, Geoffrey was found to be preparing for a night journey to London in order to catch a train there which would land him in Worcester at dawn. Because he was so clearly in no fit state for such an undertaking there were remonstrances, and he was asked why he did it. The reason, he said, was that the birthday of his eldest son fell on the morrow, and he felt he had to be there to see him wake up. The incident is symbolic of the anxious, divided life, torn between love and duty, difficult for all concerned, which was to be his and his family's until the end. Yet his home at Worcester, the house in which he settled his family after resigning St. Paul's, drew him always, and in the three sons of his marriage— Patrick, Christopher and Michael—he had deep joy. So the first of his three abiding places in these final years—Worcester, was where his heart was even though his body was condemned to the weary pilgrimage through the world which is so often the portion of the prophet.

The second, the Church of St. Edmund, King and Martyr, Lombard Street, bears to this day traces of him—a portrait in the vestry, a memorial in a side chapel, and the memory of a remarkable incumbency. The church is dark and quiet, the famous old street in which it stands surrounded by banks.

He was given the living in order that he should have time to devote himself to other things, such being the tradition of the parish, and others like it, where caretakers tended to be the only week-enders in the silent city. The pastoral demands were not heavy. Previous incumbents had been for the most part scholars and students. The fact gives a measure of what the place could be for the man holding the living: it could be what he made it. Geoffrey made it the opportunity for ceaseless, almost superhuman service. All sorts and conditions of men used to make their way to St. Edmund's when he was known to be there. That was not always: but his engagements were generally planned for him—he was hopeless at doing so himself—so that he could be at St. Edmund's usually for two Sundays in each month. And then, just as in those far away, pre-war days at St. Paul's in Worcester, people would come to him. Always a high proportion of them—and this was a very marked feature of his whole ministry—were people of no specific religious affiliation at all, but rather the doubtful, the seekers, of whom in any age there are more than meet the eye. They are not of the indifferent majority, equally, they are not of the 'faithful' who form the hard core of any Church's existence and for whom so depressingly many churches seem exclusively to exist. Rather are they the 'floating voters' of religion who, if faced with a voting card for or against belief in God would tend to place their cross in the affirmative square and then wonder wistfully if it were true. In any age these are people who will flock to that particular shepherd whose voice they seem to know, calling to them in their own half-sad, half-humorous accents. Geoffrey's was that sort of voice.

Thus it came to be remarked upon how, after a while at St. Edmund's these occasional visitors, for the most part quite unknown to the Church, came to make their Communion on the Sundays when Geoffrey was there. Their number grew until they were somewhat of an embarrassment, especially as the church was not large and had no side aisles, so that those passing to and from the altar had to do so along a centre already congested with chairs. So one of the 'faithful' was deputed to tell him about it. His reply was short: "Who am I to prevent them? How can I tell what one such contact may not mean in their lives?" Who indeed can tell? It is of the essence of such a highly personalised ministry that its effects are hidden, and vanish with the passing generations. Here some heart suddenly moved; there some eyes opened to things unseen before; a life maybe given direction. Such perhaps makes the sum of it all. But it is a considerable sum, for all that.

One feature of his services at St. Edmund's which many came to find altogether memorable was his dramatic, intense, yet exceedingly carefully prepared intercessions. "He would bring before us," wrote a woman remembering it forty years afterwards, "some one case of distress of mind or body known to him, or some national or world calamity. Then he would lead us to see such things as incidents in a battle between good and evil that was always going on. When he did this it was strange how one forgot one's self concerns altogether. And after that, in a complete quiet, he would ask us to remain absolutely still and allow ourselves to become the channels by which God might work His will through to that particular situation." There were many elsewhere, who met him during retreats and missions, who remembered this oddly intense intercession more clearly than anything else. It was an experience, though at times it could be startling, as when, during the General Strike, politicians and trades union leaders were presented severally by name, with considerable biographical detail, to the prayers of the congregation.

Such methods require very special powers in the executor if they are not to topple over into absurdity. It is true that there were always some who thought that Geoffrey was unduly histrionic. But at least that was natural: he was a histrionic person, a fact very evident in his preaching, although there it was a small element in a far greater whole. The fact is that in these years of campaigning for the I.C.F., constantly exercising his art, those rare gifts came to the full fruition which had been noticed many years ago in Geoffrey when first his oratorical genius began to emerge.

What, then, were the elements which made up Geoffrey's preaching? Here is a matter worth looking at in a day when the very art itself seems to be dwindling away. That shrewd journalist, Sidney Dark, who in his day strayed so surprisingly from Fleet Street to the *Church Times*, went so far as to say: "I imagine that no religious leader since General Booth has had so great a popular appeal. I heard S.K. once in the Dome at Brighton. The great hall was crammed to the back of the gallery. The preliminary speakers were heard with a certain impatience, and there was a curious rustle of expectation when the little dark man in his cassock stepped to the table. For a minute or so he knelt in quiet prayer, and then he began to talk, and he talked in what were actually burning sentences. He was indeed an orator of genius. He went easily from grave to gay; he played on his audience as an organist plays on an organ. He was an inspired demagogue in the best sense of that term."[1]

But the effect, he adds, was due to the quivering sincerity of the man even more than to any conscious art. Such was the impression given; such no doubt was the impression Geoffrey sought to give. But in fact there was a great deal of conscious art about

[1] *Church Times*, March 20th, 1929.

Geoffrey's preaching. It was indeed no more artless than the performance of a great pianist. "He lived in a state of fierce indignation against the cruelties and injustices of modern life, and this came through," Dark added, and that, of course, was true enough. So a sense of purpose, a conviction of an adversary to be fought, was certainly a prime element in Geoffrey's preaching. A further one was an extraordinarily vivid feeling for Christ as a person, terribly closely involved in the whole drama of human life, just as Geoffrey had found him to be so on the battle-fields. And the strength of this feeling within himself enabled him at times to evoke it in others to an astonishing degree.

On Good Fridays in Dick Sheppard's time, Mr. Arthur Bourchier would put the Strand Theatre at the disposal of the Vicar of St. Martin's. A grey ticket of admission to the Three Hours' Service on one such Good Friday of the early twenties announces Geoffrey as the speaker. What happened is told by a cutting from the *Morning Post* of the following day. "On the stage, throughout the whole of the time, stood the priest, burning with nervous zeal. Men—there were hundreds of them—and women sat as if hypnotised, moved often to tears, held prisoner by the eloquence of a man whose soul was on fire. The stage was at length, towards the end, invaded."

This in a London theatre in the middle of the day in an age scarcely notable for fervour of any sort. It makes a strange picture. One wonders if it could ever be repeated. But it was equalled often and often in these closing years of Geoffrey's life. American tours he made under the auspices of the Berkeley Divinity School in the mid-twenties led to similar scenes. "I heard him first at the Indianapolis Convention of the Student Volunteers in 1923. He electrified that vast audience," wrote one who was there. And again; "He came to the seminary at Alexandria, Virginia, where I was a student. I can see him now standing in the chapel wearing one of the professor's gowns which was way too long for him, and picking up the skirt and wrapping it round his arms as he spoke— wrapping and unwrapping this black gown with red facings. He gave a talk which I can remember still, and his voice saying; 'One of my earliest recollections is of my mother reading to me in a soft Irish brogue the opening words of *Pilgrim's Progress*.' He quoted it, and I remember still his pronunciation of the word 'lamentable'. 'He broke into a *lar*mentable cry.' "[1]

To most who heard him his speaking appeared to be brilliantly extempore. In fact, it was nothing of the sort. Meticulous preparation backed by a powerful memory was of the essence of it. He once said he 'dared leave nothing to chance'. Most of his set-piece orations were committed entirely to memory so thoroughly that he could, and frequently did, transpose whole sections verbatim. The same American who heard him often soon discovered this : "I became aware that he combined elements from many sermons in different ways according to circumstances; but the passages, though variously arranged, were always the same in content. This taught me much about his preaching method."

Geoffrey's memory, so vague in many ways, was certainly phenomenal in this respect. His secretary noted how, once he had dictated a speech to her, he had only to read through the typescript once to become word-perfect. He would go to the meeting without notes. But she, following him from the script, marked how his words followed the text line by line. Everything was there, even the apparently casual interjections. This was his art; he excelled in it. But the

[1] Private information.

price paid in labour was enormous, and it was scarcely surprising that those—and they were numerous—who tried to emulate his style so often failed not only because they lacked his unique fire, but also because they fell short of the rigorous preparation which was the price of its effectiveness.

Kirk of I.C.F. also noted something of this care in preparation. Geoffrey's method, as he observed it, was to write his addresses on a pad which he carried with him and would work upon as occasion offered. If he made one correction on a sheet, he rewrote it all immediately. Ultimately, he had the whole off by heart. Every phrase, which in the hearing seemed so spontaneous, had a fixed, predetermined place, and the whole was delivered with enormous energy, humour, and raciness which some found distasteful, exactly as some had found it so during the war years. He spoke usually for at least an hour —on one occasion for two, quite carried away, and disturbed afterwards to find he had been so long. But his audience had been held.

In these years, his resting-place—often his only one —was the train, and he was not always left undisturbed there. One of the headquarters staff of I.C.F. remembered travelling with him to a crusade on a train which happened also to be returning from a race-meeting. The two of them had to squeeze into a compartment where a card game was in progress. Gradually silence fell as Geoffrey, quite unconscious of his surroundings, continued the discussion—one of the endless argument he loved—which he and his companion had been having on the platform. Then one of the card-players, who had heard that voice before, not so many years back, muttered to his neighbour, "Woodbine—" The name was enough. By the end of the journey they were all arguing together.

But the flavour of these years was for the most part a bitter one. At the end of Geoffrey's day, men from the Rhondda were singing *Jesu Lover of my soul*, in the London gutters while the red buses blew exhaust at them. That was only one aspect of the disjointedness of the times. God knows, there were plenty of others. But it was the one which affected Geoffrey the most deeply, and with which his work for the I.C.F. brought him into closest touch. "His passionate concern for the down-and-outs has probably done more to arouse public conscience than all the endless discussions in Parliament," P. T. R. Kirk considered, "for he taught by example as well as by precept. He had the human touch, if ever a man had it; and bore in his body the marks of the Lord Jesus. There was a world of sorrow in his deep eyes."

But if all this was bitter-flavoured, he could yet find sweetness in the personal contacts which his work involved. The headquarters staff of I.C.F. he loved dearly. The General Director, Kirk, accepted the living of Christ Church, Westminster, in 1922, and it was in the vicarage there throughout these years that a room was always kept for Geoffrey and companionship and guidance offered when, as was often, he needed both. The guidance was something he had always needed. Now, without Kirk, he might well have become an unguided missile of evangelism, just as Kirk without him might have been a man with a message lacking the means of projecting it upon the world. As it was, the two complemented each other. And if Geoffrey was able to do more than any other man of his generation to commend the Gospel in the Market Place and the factories of his day and age, and if I.C.F. was a power for good, it was due in no small measure to the fact that these two were close friends, brothers in the work. That did not prevent Geoffrey from being worked remorselessly hard; but the cause was a great one, and in any event he was a man born to burn rather than rust out. There was also Miss E. C. Knight-Bruce, Geoffrey's opposite number as a woman messenger for the Fellowship, whose handsome features look out from I.C.F. group photographs of the period. She had, it was said, in addition to presence and formidable intelligence, a lovely voice, and would sing Geoffrey's sentimental verses, put to music by the organist of St. Edmund's, Lombard Street—"When through the whirl of wheels and engines humming—"

This is the verse which speaks of the miner, far below ground 'wielding his pick more splendid than the sword', and of the second coming of the Lord:

> God in a workman's jacket as before,
> Living again the eternal Gospel story,
> Sweeping the shavings from his workshop floor.

The sentimentality, the idealisation of labour, all bring back Geoffrey and his day. However, it was easier then to see Christ in the worker, when that worker was so obviously, it seemed, being once again the victim of economic theory.

And then again there was Alice Charles, for twenty years Director of Studies. She it was who wrote of Geoffrey:

"To me, as a teacher, what I admired most was the wonderful gift he had of expressing the most profound dogmatic truths in language that could be understood and appreciated by simple and unlearned people. This is obvious in his writings, but when the stuff in his books was delivered by him in his addresses —as it generally was—backed by his powerful personality and his intense desire to bring men to Christ, and his complete self-dedication, it availed greatly. In the mass meetings and open-airs which he addressed, there were many who took their first steps towards the Christian faith through him.

"No one who worked with him in the Crusades will ever forget the urgency of the crowds by which he was surrounded in the cities and squares, nor the vast length and eagerness of the queues that waited to get into his mass meetings. The Holy Ghost was truly there to 'inspire and lighten with celestial fire'."[1]

Such people were a few among many; but they did happen to be among those who were able to observe Geoffrey at close quarters. It is clear that the staff adored him, to whom his general helplessness in the practical affairs of life could make a powerful appeal. It was a long-remembered excitement to have to help him out when he turned up penniless, or to see him coming in with a huge toy in his arms for one of his children, or to encounter some of the incredible people who came looking for him in Westminster; that Queen of the Tarts already mentioned, or some of the ex-prisoners from Wandsworth who came after he had visited the prison and offered help to anyone who, on release, felt in need of it, or to listen to him in theological argument with Miss Knight-Bruce during some long journey. Now the tale of that particular day is finished. But among such memories of small things which are still to be detected around the scene, like some previous occupant's scent in the wardrobe of an hotel bedroom, is still to be found something of that extraordinary warming of the heart which Geoffrey was able to inspire. As with those who knew him long ago in Leeds and Rugby and Worcester, and France, so now it was with these who encountered him in his last years, that they felt something very remarkable, something very moving, had been glimpsed passing upon the usually grey highway of life. And

[1] Private information.

when he was able, as he often was, to lift up their hearts in his retreat addresses, the impression was deepened. Thus Kirk, of just such an occasion in 1923:

"The talks given to a little company at a retreat at High Leigh were unforgettable. One who was there writes of the setting of glorious spring weather—sunshine and a blaze of flowers. His message seemed to be a part of their setting. He sat in the big chair of the chapel, looking past his hearers to the glory of the garden."

What was he saying? This is one of the far too rare occasions when we can know, because his notes have survived. He would be looking out on the flowers Kirk speaks of when he said: 'He maketh me lie down in green pastures: He leadeth me beside still waters.' This is a picture of beauty: the shepherd wandering with his sheep to the quiet pool through the green and gold of nature—the pool exceedingly still, with shadows in its heart. But the sheep follow the shepherd, not because of the beauty; but because they are hungry. So if we crave beauty, it must be not as a luxury but as a necessity: if we follow the shepherd it must be from necessity. God is never real until he is just that."

He certainly craved beauty himself. Among Kirk's memories is one of Geoffrey, on the first visit to the Alps, having to be sought until at last found, quite overcome by the tremendous spectacle of those 'snowy summits old in story'. Many have felt the same, of course; the only exceptional feature of this sort of reaction was its intensity. But the importance of the matter to Geoffrey's thinking lay in the fact that he so emphatically identified God with such outward phenomena, thus laying himself open to the charge of pantheism often brought against him. A man who could say, as he did, that there was the Kingdom

and the Power and the Glory in the towers of York
and Bach's *Mass in B Minor* was obviously rendering
himself vulnerable.

But to get back to the train—Geoffrey's movements
had to be carefully planned not only because he was
liable to forget date, destination and purpose of journeys; but also because there were so many of them.
So generally he would be issued with a list stretching
far into the future—during one Crusade there was a
man charged with the sole duty of getting him to
the right place at the right time. One such list, still
extant, presents a picture of him being shunted cease-
lessly from one end of the country to another, from
the Rotarians of Warrington, to a mission at Barry, to
a mass meeting in Carlisle, to Leicester Cathedral, to
Liverpool Cathedral to St. Mary's, Oxford, to the Town
Hall, Wallasey, the Brighton Corn Exchange, to un-
counted churches, a miner's demonstration in Durham,
and to some long-forgotten, unspecified, curiosity-
arousing meeting with persons unknown in the middle
of the afternoon in a theatre in Swanage. Such became
the common form of his life. But the great occasions,
those which showed both him and the work to which
he had devoted himself at fullest stretch, came when
a train delivered him at the station of some town for
the beginning of that characteristic activity of the
I.C.F. of the time—the Crusade.

It is certainly true that such things have been common in all ages to the history of religion. It may well
be equally true that their ashes can rarely be stirred
with profit. A mission, a campaign, is held; many
words are spoken, a varying degree of warmth is en-
gendered. Then it is over, the fire dies down, and the
winds of everyday appear to blow as coolly as ever
over an unchanged scene. But sometimes—not often,
perhaps, but sometimes—it is different; the fire does

not die wholly away, but can be found years after-
wards still glowing comfortingly in a few private lives.
And that at least can be claimed for some of these
I.C.F. crusades.

The time was apt for the invigorating exposition
of the Christian faith in relation to social, economic
and political life. There was need to get out into the
streets and talk about Christ the Lord of All Life when
he seemed so singularly absent from the discouraging
scene. What is more, it was still possible in that time,
before radio and television had altered social habits
in these respects to gather people together in large
masses. Above all, these Crusades of the twenties,
though they represented, and were made possible by,
the labours of many, had in Geoffrey a central figure
of genius, while the economic tragedy of the times
gave them vivid relevance. These factors together made
possible results, in terms of fervour and enduring inspiration, which even at this distance of time are surprising.

Geoffrey was involved in many such Crusades. They
were always carefully prepared, the process beginning
perhaps a year beforehand with local committees of
clergy and business men co-operating with the I.C.F.
priest director and headquarters staff in arranging the
programme. By the time the Crusaders themselves arrived the ground would have been thoroughly made
ready for the 'ploughing-up' which was intended.
The Crusaders themselves invariably included I.C.F.
missioners who had been working-men themselves.
These were always a very important feature of the
whole enterprise, and represented, more than anything else, the element of continuance in the work of
I.C.F. In addition there would be four or five clergy
accustomed to the rigours of open-air speaking, a number of women and the Crusade leader, often a bishop,

sometimes, in his day, Geoffrey himself. And also special speakers would be brought in—George Lansbury was one, Sir William Cash another, and Christian economists, employers, trade union leaders. The whole effort would last a week or two, gradually building up to the climax of mass-meetings towards the end. Meanwhile there would have been daily factory and canteen gatherings in the lunch-hour, and at night—most challenging of all—open-air pitches for the proclamation of the Crusade message and for the uninhibited and at times bitter debate of bitter times.

The message of a crusade was based on the syllabus drawn up in the early years of I.C.F., *Christ the Lord of All Life*. Geoffrey had a hand in this clear exposition of Christian fundamentals. To read it is to realise at once how far removed these Crusades were from the kind of mission, often focused upon the personality of one man, which in recent times appears to have taken up the torch of emotional evangelism.

Here is something quite different. Even the purpose of the Crusades differed utterly from the "decision for Christ" objective of a later day. "It is an endeavour," the book stated, "to present the Christian religion to the people of a town or district as the solution of the problem of modern social life as they see and experience it . . . The appeal to the individual is made to him as a member of society. A Crusade endeavours to give this message to those whom the Church does not otherwise reach . . . It does not aim directly at getting people into the Church, though that has sometimes happened to a considerable extent; but it offers a magnificent opportunity for the removal of deep-seated misconceptions, and for putting truer ways of thinking before people who have hitherto left organised religion altogether out of account."

Emphasis was laid also upon the importance of

meeting people upon their own ground, of starting from the known and going on to the unknown. Above all, speakers were urged to have constantly in mind that principle at the heart of all successful communication—a principle so often forgotten or ignored—of speaking in a language that could be understood. Conventional religious phrases were to be avoided at all costs. "We have to aim at presenting the truth in all its depth and power, but in quite a different sort of language." It was a task exactly suited to Geoffrey's genius. Many shared it with him; but these many were the first to recognise how overwhelmingly much whatever success the enterprise had, owed to him.

These dry bones came together into life, each day having its theme, and each theme having its place in the message as a whole, so that from a beginning at the contemporary order of society, its origins, its evils and its challenges, the argument passed on by stages to the relevance of Christ and his Church and to the common life which had to be lived therein. Above all, personal contacts were made often during the course of a Crusade, some of which can be found having their effect to this day.

In the middle twenties a train deposited Geoffrey at the city of Stoke in the Potteries. This was the scene of a notable Crusade, perhaps the greatest of his time. Indeed, for many years afterwards an annual service used to be held in those unlovely places, Tunstall, Hanley and Longton, commemorating the effort, as though it had been a battle. There, in the six towns with their potbanks, the iron and steel works at Shelton Bar, and the collieries around, was a fit setting for an effort symbolised in the poster which had been visible around the area for some time past. It showed the tower of Hanley Parish Church shrouded in the smoke of potbanks curling up to the legend

"Is it nothing to you, all ye that pass by?" In the event, it turned out to be much. The interest, even the passion aroused, was enormous. One who was there, as curate of Stoke in those days, remembered how.

"Each day the missioners, about eighty of them, met in Hanley Old Church. Bishop Kempthorne of Lichfield, was leader, but it was S.K. who gave the message for the day. In this he excelled. Many people crowded into this meeting just to hear him . . . Every evening, in one of the Town Halls, there was a mass meeting, often representing some industrial interest. S.K. was a necessity here. There was a dinner-hour meeting every day in Stoke Parish Church, which held two thousand. It was packed daily—for S.K. My last and most distinct memory of him was on the last Sunday, in Hanley, after the evening services. The Victoria Hall had been set aside, and the largest Methodist Church had been added. Both were packed. I sat on the floor in the Victoria Hall at the edge of the platform. It was like that."[1]

Geoffrey, it seemed, spoke first at the Methodist Church, an all-out effort. He then had to face the crowd waiting in the Victoria Hall and repeat the whole thing. He was exhausted by the ten previous days. By the time he reached this final meeting he was; "visibly reeling with fatigue. How he kept on his feet I don't know, but he kept on till he had done his work. I cannot describe the impression he made in that Crusade, except to say that he was the best-known man in the place, and continued to be a name for many years after."

As always where Geoffrey was involved the memories surviving are a mixture of the absurd and the touching. So one will recall touring the 'pitches' with him and seeing, as it grew dark, the light of a street-

[1] Private information.

lamp on his face while questions came out of the shadows. "He always answered on the level of the questioner, but going deeper as he went on, until there was silence all around." Or again a man coming shyly up to him in a similar dusk scene, some private words passing between them, and Geoffrey afterwards saying to the helper doing the rounds of the 'pitches' with him, "He was at Messines." Or again Geoffrey startling a gathering of Potteries business-men in boiled shirts by opening an after-dinner speech, after a long look round the tables with the words; "My God, but it's funny, the kind of people he allows to have money!" Or again, but this time in a pulpit, in the brogue he put on with such ease. "David in his haste said all men were liars. If he'd taken his time he'd have said it just the same." This, of course, was the kind of thing which had so annoyed General Plumer and others, years before. It continued to annoy. Clergy especially started with a prejudice against him. But, as Bishop Kempthorne recorded of this Stoke crusade, they were soon won over by his obvious humility and the reality of his spiritual power. And then, as always, there were a great number of individuals who came to him for personal counsel. "I remember one time," is another memory, "that he had so many to see him after a meeting that when he came in he was so exhausted he literally could not speak—"

And the results? Who can say? Who can now presume even to try to measure so insubstantial, so gossamer-like a quality? The thing is secret, and perhaps should be, unless the whole business is to sink to the level of that kind of evangelism which counts the number of the alleged converted as a brave once reckoned his scalps. There was nothing of that, either in atmosphere or intention, about these I.C.F. Crusades of the twenties. In any case, the only results of any value, in this as in any other kind of high endeavour, are those which last. Whether, when the excitement had died down, and the missioners had departed, any abiding impression had been made, may well be difficult to decide. Even so, it is something to discover for how many years the effect endured of the Stoke Crusade, to take that one instance alone. Thus there was the manufacturer to whose heart, in some way or another the whole thing, and Geoffrey especially, spoke direct, and who as a consequence tried down all the years since to run his great concern on Christian principles. And then again there was the stout-hearted man who was appointed full-time missioner to carry on the work, and did so, for many years, until other times and other manners rendered it all less meaningful. 'Is it nothing to you, all ye that pass by?' the poster advertising the Stoke Crusade had asked. Perhaps it was enough that there were some at least who found, as a result of it all, and of the many efforts like it, that a little light was cast thereby upon the business of living.

It was during this Stoke Crusade that the same man who watched Geoffrey's supreme effort during the packed final meeting noticed how each morning, while the day's business was being arranged, he was to be seen in a corner, abstracted amid the surrounding noise, quietly writing. The book was *The Wicket Gate*. With the other product of these I.C.F. years, *The Word and the Work* it represents, apart from his verse, the most important writing he managed to distil from the pressures of an absurdly overcrowded life. It is a brilliant demonstration of the art of communication of basic truths in the language of the kind of person for whom it was intended—that 'plain man' with his inarticulate longings and unanswered questions who, as Geoffrey passionately felt, usually found precious little of satisfaction to his soul in organised religion as he commonly encountered it. Yet his needs were great for 'the plain bread of religion which a man must have in order to live'. It is a bad time for the man in the street. He is aware he dwells in the City of Destruction . . . In the unutterable depths of his inarticulate soul there is trouble, and he breaks out with a lamentable cry saying, *What shall I do?* . . . We cannot see the wicket-gate, or walk in the narrow way of our forefathers: and to the ancient Evangelist who kindly points it out, we can only answer 'No!' But when he further says, 'Do you see yonder shining light?' there are thousands who would reply doubt-fully, hesitatingly, and yet with a thrill of hope, 'I think I do'." So Geoffrey wrote in his introduction.

Such thousands are still around, of course. And they are certainly more conscious, and with reason, of being in the City of Destruction. And here, at this very point, is the importance of Geoffrey for today. To read these two books of his now is often to be aston-ished at their topicality. Thus, in *The Word and the Work*:

"European man, whom the Dean of St. Paul's des-cribes as 'the fiercest of the beasts of prey, who is not likely to abandon the weapons which have made him the lord and bully of the planet, is threatened with extinction unless he becomes either a more tyr-annous lord, using without restraint or remorse the powers of destruction that have been put into his hands, or dies with Christ, and finds a more excellent way."

That 'more excellent way', in *The Wicket Gate* on the basis of the Lord's Prayer, in *The Word and the Work* on the Logos passage of St. John, is tellingly set forth, pleaded for, given contemporary signifi-cance. Both books arose directly out of Geoffrey's constant confrontation with the spiritual problems of people outside the enclosing walls of churches. As a consequence, both books seem quite exceptionally real, in the sense of lighting up questions which belong to the very stuff of existence. Both cry aloud for quotation; both are rich in aphorism, which together suggest formidable qualities. Thus, in *The Word and the Work*:

"The world and the life of men have meaning and purpose. At its heart the world is not mad; but sane. That is the bare minimum of faith for man. If that goes, everything goes, and we can neither live nor think about life; but only take a long time to die."

Or again; "Nobody worries about Christ as long as he can be kept shut up in churches. He is quite safe there. But there is always trouble if you try to let him out."

Or once again, from *The Wicket Gate*:

"However difficult it may be—and it is difficult— to see and to realise the unity of the secular and the sacred, it remains true that to see it and to realise it is the essence of religion."

"This book will make people *think*," the Bishop of London said of *The Word and the Work*. It was a true judgment, still valid. The pity is that there were not more books of Geoffrey's. For the need is still great in every generation for the very special kind of approach which they represent, at once exciting and illuminating, to the vast army of those who are yet prepared to see 'yonder shining light' if only there is someone to point it out to them across the wide field of human experience.

The other two books Geoffrey managed, somehow, to produce are of lesser calibre altogether. He was right in saying, as he did in the introduction to it, that *The Warrior, the Woman and the Christ* bit off more than it could chew. The result is confused. He was attempting to think aloud over the fact that "the traditions, the habits, the conventions which surround the relation of the sexes are all breaking up, and we have nothing to put in their place". The impression is of someone attempting to cover so wide a ground of speculation that sight is lost of the original point of departure. Thus a book which begins at the fact of sex—a fact with which he admits to have been himself preoccupied for years—and of which many had spoken to him 'not a few in tears' in the course of his pastoral ministry, is soon talking about the 'Creative Conflict'. It does not quite come off, even though the justification of this discursiveness is significant. No thinking about sex, he maintains, can be straight thinking if the subject is considered in isolation from the rest of experience. When it is, it becomes an obsession. So his book is about everything, including God and the universe, because the sexual factor is itself a part of everything, including God and the universe. Much subsequent literature of sex, which has tended so often to regard the subject in clinical isolation, might well have benefited by recognition of this basic fact. But Geoffrey was before his time in this, as in other things.

His one and only novel *I Pronounce Them* sprang from one aspect of the same theme. He wrote it, he said, because he had to. And the reason for this inner compulsion lay in the many questionings which had sprung up in his mind regarding the whole nature of Christian marriage and the problems arising from its sometimes inevitable failures. "No one has really faced the problem of the 'innocent party'," he wrote, "until he has been faced with a man or woman whom he knows and loves, and been asked to decide what God's will is in their particular case . . . I have had to stand it many times, and been sick with doubt." So indeed have many other priests. So have many other men and women broken on the wheel of rigorism. The theme was a great one. Geoffrey felt passionately about it. But clearly the writing of novels was not his line. Robert Paterson, the respectable clergyman in a cathedral town which is a thinly disguised Worcester, and Jim Counihan, his friend and fellow parson who, with his "very large head, enormous dark eyes, and ugly face" is not even thinly disguised, do not as characters convince. And the plot, with its problem-demonstrating situations; Counihan's wife asking for divorce; his own desire to re-marry, and the presentation of similar problems in other characters on other levels result in a tract rather than a novel. Even so, it has its moments. The argument over the ethics of contraception in the vicarage study, with the doctor and the social worker looking with affectionate bewilderment upon a troubled parson opposing, because he feels the Church requires him to, the establishment of a family-planning clinic in his parish, faithfully reflects the process by which the Church over the years has been brought, if reluctantly, to a sensible and humane view of this matter.

But what chiefly impresses about this honest, rather groping tale told, as Geoffrey said, "by a fool striving to help his fellow fools, and to guide their sorely wounded feet into the way of peace;" is at once its modernity and its courage. With its frank—a word not then as prostituted as now—revelation of problems still at that time by custom concealed; adultery, abortion, illicit love often truer than licit, the basic dishonesty of many social attitudes towards sex and marriage, it was far ahead of its time. It was something, after all, to put a foot through one of the windows which for so long, as in the sick-room of a Victorian consumptive, had been keeping fresh air from an unhealthy sector of society. *I Pronounce Them*, bad novel as it may have been, did just that. It was very popular, even reaching the stage in an adaptation at the Everyman Theatre.

Such, then, were the books of these years, written in snatches any time, anywhere, as the train trundled him about the country. He grew increasingly exhausted, increasingly indifferent to the many warnings that he was killing himself. "I took him to poverty-stricken Abertillery," wrote one who encountered him during a South Wales crusade, "there I left him, after he had walked through a crowded hall, mounted the platform, looked at his audience, and began: 'Are you afraid of poverty?' Ninety minutes later, when I returned from another meeting to collect him, he still held the gathering entranced. He had had no evening meal, and it was getting late. He glanced at a message I sent to the stage to say I was ready to take him to his lodgings, and continued. I sent another message. When he finished, some thirty minutes later, I strode to the platform. He was surrounded with people getting his autograph.

"I took him, another day, to a mountain-side to address a huge open-air meeting. Without amplifying aids he spoke to the multitude. For two hours he got down to the root of things, in a district heading for Communism. On the way back, I tried to stop a man from forcing his way into the car. S.K. needed the opportunity for quiet. S.K. invited him in — and they talked all the way . . ."

"Wandering like Satan among the sons of men," he wrote in the Visitor's Book of the Toc H hostel where, gasping with asthma, he spent the ensuing night.

And what did it all amount to? The question can be asked about any human endeavour, and a disparaging reply is always possible. That is particularly the case, perhaps, in this whole matter of the Christian conscience and the economic order. "It is difficult, looking back—and casting aside the martyrs' crowns that have been posthumously awarded—to think that the Church's social protest in the inter-war years was anything more than a product of a sense of personal shame and financial guilt."[1]

A martyr's crown? Such a thing, as Geoffrey might well have said with one of his grins, would have looked most peculiar on his oversize head. In any event the social protest of the Church was always a periphery activity of that body, however hard William Temple might strive to move it nearer the centre. And always there was the vast, circumambient indifference of the world to contend with. Geoffrey knew, as few have known, what that meant, because he had the prophet's eyes to see. This is what he wrote of it, in a poem which, summing up the experience of these closing years of his life, beyond all others, catches the profound and mysterious sadness lying for him at the heart of things. At Golgotha, he says, men at least crucified Christ. But:

When Jesus came to Birmingham they simply passed him by,
They never hurt a hair of him, they simply let him die;
For men had grown more tender, and they would not give him pain,
They only just passed down the street, and left him in the rain.
Still Jesus cried, "Forgive them, for they know not what they do",
And still it rained the wintry rain that drenched him through and through;

[1] Anthony Howard—in *The Baldwin Age*. Eyre & Spottiswoode. 1960.

The crowds went home and left the streets without
a soul to see,
And Jesus crouched against a wall and cried for
Calvary.

Did Geoffrey sometimes cry for his own? There
were many among those who encountered him towards the end of the twenties who had the impression of him as of a man who would welcome release,
when it came, from the burden of life which had
become too heavy, too exacting, too saddened by the
insights of a prophet, by the constant wear and tear
of an uprooted, hard-driven, anxious existence which
would have tried to the limit a physique far stronger
than Geoffrey's ever was. However, as it happened,
release was very close, by the winter of 1928.

CHAPTER VII

'THAT'S ALL'

ONE morning early in the March of 1929 Geoffrey
came out of his house in Worcester, *en route* for the
station and a train for Liverpool. At the gate he hesi-
tated, then re-entered the house. His wife and the
children were all down with 'flu. He was ill himself;
weary to the bone, stricken with the asthma which
had dogged him through the years. And now he was
nagged by the anxiety of leaving the family sick. He
went upstairs; looked down at his wife, asking her
if she could manage; if he should go. Half reassured,
a moment later he left the house, and this time did
not turn back. He had begun his last journey. A few
days later, in the early hours of Friday, March 8th, in
a bedroom at St. Catherine's Vicarage, Abercromby
Square, Liverpool, he died.

178

Of course, he should not have set out. But then, there were many things he should not have done, for years past, if ever he were to know fullness of days. Yet for him any self-saving, anything other than an utter self-giving, was out of character. He had to burn out, like one of the Verey lights of the old front, in the old war. And now his light was arcing down in the last moments of its trajectory, before being swallowed up forever in the darkness. He had for some time past been well aware he was nearing his limits. "Worn out; but not worked out" was how he described himself. And speaking at Wallasey for the last time from a public platform, he had ended with the words:

> Christ, though my hands be bleeding,
> Fierce though my flesh be pleading,
> Still let me see thee leading,
> Let me build on!

He had gone to Liverpool to give a series of Lenten addresses at Liverpool Parish Church, but soon had to take to his bed. By the Thursday, although very ill, he was holding on. But then, quite suddenly, the tired heart finally gave in. Mrs. Studdert Kennedy, summoned from Worcester, travelled through the night only to find him unconscious at her arrival. By dawn he had gone. The press of Saturday, March 9th, reflected a sorrow quite extraordinary in its intensity.

One thing became immediately apparent. Geoffrey had been a national figure to a degree which would probably have astonished him more than anyone else. The fact was soon made plain—touchingly, surprisingly so. A decent regret usually attends the passing of the captains and the kings of this world. The right, the expected things are said, the dignitaries of a formal mourning are observed from afar by the passing crowds. Only occasionally does a death seem to draw from those crowds themselves some special reaction, expressed in simple emotional acts.

The obsequies of Geoffrey, which were elaborate and prolonged, gave rise to many instances of such.

They began in Liverpool itself, when his body was taken from the vicarage to St. Catherine's church to lie before the altar. Throughout that Friday some two thousand people of all sorts and conditions, including a coloured man wearing his war-medals, passed through the church. The following morning two hundred were at the early celebration. Afterwards, at the removal of the coffin for its journey to Worcester, some man unknown stepped forward to lay a packet of Woodbines on it, and passengers on the ferry by which it was taken across the river were moved to take part in a short service before the boat set out. At Worcester the body was taken to St. Paul's in Geoffrey's old parish, where the streets were packed to receive it, and where, among those who kept continuous watch by the coffin through night as well as day, were many of those drawn from the characteristic army of the period—the unemployed. A detachment of these, mustered at the Labour Exchange, marched in the enormous funeral procession which left the Cathedral, whither Geoffrey's body had in the meanwhile been taken, on the following Tuesday.

That was a funeral long remembered in Worcester; the silent streets, the shuttered shops, the crowds lining the route all the two miles to the cemetery; the wreaths with the sentimental notes: 'To a fallen comrade'; 'To Woodbine Willie'; 'To a man'. There were hundreds of them. And perhaps these, for all their crudity, were nearer the true nature of the man to whom they sought to pay tribute than the royal telegram which expressed the King's sympathy. The same could be said of the memorial services. There was a distinguished one at St. Martin in the Fields, another at Liverpool Cathedral, another at Bristol, another at Manchester. There was also one held, for some reason or other, maybe because of some warm memory he had left there, at Risca, in a South Wales deep in the depression. There was a parade on that occasion of a scout troop; 'Woodbine Willie's Own', and it is possible to feel that this among them all would most have appealed to Geoffrey.

But the world had not quite finished with him yet. After the funeral, after the memorial services, there was still some clearing-up to be done. The family, for one thing, was left in a difficult situation. There were two younger sons still to be educated and, though Geoffrey from his writings had in his final years made a fair income, he had given most of it away. This habit had never ceased. When at St. Edmunds he had been given a cheque for £200 as an Easter gift, he gave it immediately, somewhat to the indignation of the donors, to the Miners' Distress fund then in operation. Such property as he did possess he left, in a will written on the torn-off page of a field service notebook, to his wife. But he had at least been rich in friends, some of whom, including Temple of York, Davidson of Lambeth, and Kirk of the Industrial Christian Fellowship, launched a memorial fund appeal. They asked for £7,000; they received more, and one of the first to respond was the King. After that, here and there, memorial tablets appeared. That in Worcester Cathedral says all there is to say:

"Geoffrey Anketell Studdert Kennedy, M.C., a poet; a prophet, a passionate seeker after truth; an ardent advocate of Christian fellowship, Chaplain to H.M. King George V, Chaplain to the Forces, Rector of St.

Edmunds King and Martyr in the City of London, sometime Vicar of St. Paul's in this city. Born 27 June 1883, died March 8, 1929."

Meanwhile, there had been appearing in the press at home and abroad a great number of appreciations of Geoffrey. Most of them were endeavours to approach somewhere near the truth of what his essential nature had been, and it is clear that many of the writers found the undertaking difficult. The problem was to find points of comparison. Thus the Bishop of Kensington, preaching at the memorial service at St. Martin's: "He was quite unlike anyone else. He combined in his personality so many striking elements that there was in him something entirely original . . ."

What was it? That is the basic question, and it has never been answered. Perhaps it never can be answered, even though it is a matter of import, even fascination, since here was one who somehow seemed able, without for a moment getting his feet off the ground, to testify to the absolute reality and the absolute relevance of God. Partly, maybe, the answer lay in his insight into the truth that sacred and secular are one, so that no one in fact lives on the one side or the other of a fence dividing one from the other. There is no fence. So he was able, to a rare degree, to see God in all things, to see the divine, revealed in the common things of life, giving to all a dignity and significance.

But thus to define one of his master ideas—which in any event was not peculiar to him—is not to draw much nearer that absolute originality of which the Bishop of Kensington spoke. Certainly, he fitted into no ecclesiastical mould. "He was much more than a great Churchman," said *The Daily News*, "if indeed he really was that at all: he was a great Christian." And *The Scots Observer* well expressed the difficulties of tying any labels on him when it said: "To many of his friends he was a constant enigma. They disliked much of the freedom which he took with language and ideas; but the love which bubbled over from his heart they could not but love in return." Even so, there were revealing things written of him. Kirk, Dick Sheppard, F. R. Barry, and J. K. Mozley, each had something to contribute to the task of trying to form an overall picture of him. Kirk especially, spoke of two aspects of Geoffrey's character which seemed so oddly contrasted; the pugnacity which made him relish putting plain truths into plain words without fear of the often considerable consequences, and a "Franciscan simplicity, a wedding to purity, a kinship with all created things which endeared him to all who knew him as the same qualities endeared the Saint of Assisi to his friends." Kirk wrote as one who had loved Geoffrey greatly, so some partiality may be allowed. But the article does contain one very significant quotation from the last article Geoffrey had written for the I.C.F. journal—a passage which gives some indication of the price in mental and spiritual tension which had to be paid, which had for years been paid by him, in the ceaseless attempt to measure his faith against the facts of life as he saw them. "Every man, whether Christian or not, must sooner or later stand in the last ditch face to face with the final doubt. I know that last ditch well. I have stood in it many a time; and I know that before I die I shall stand there again—and again."

Both Barry and Mozley stressed the element of the prophet in Geoffrey, and perhaps it is here that the true source of his originality is to be found. The true prophet, as Mozley said, is a student of life who penetrates to its meaning in the light of the knowledge of God. The definition fitted Geoffrey exactly. But there was more to it than that. "The true prophet," Mozley added, "is one who sees life truly and does not speak smooth things to obscure the truth. He of whom we are thinking saw most truly one of the profoundest facts of life—its continual tension in all human relations, which inevitably involves the presence of suffering . . . He gave no easy message; his sympathy for all sufferers cost him dear; but he never suggested that there was any means of evading the tension, conflict and suffering of life . . . Geoffrey Studdert Kennedy did not spare himself. He bore the pain of his unflinching, open-eyed struggle to penetrate to the heart of things . . . His sole concern was with facts as they are, and against them he sought no protection."

It was true also that his message seemed to come upon him from 'outside'. Many commentators made this point. Often he seemed possessed, used as an instrument by a force which he shrank from because it exhausted him so utterly. His friends dreaded the effects of these visitations upon him. However, as Barry said, "When God raises up a prophet for us, we do not stone him or persecute him; we either ignore him or kill him with overwork." And Geoffrey was never ignored. "Too little has been written," was Dick Sheppard's conclusion to a moving appreciation in *The Times*, "about this great and good man who could fill the largest hall in England. Those who went to hear him would never have come away saying merely 'What an orator!' They would have been conscious of having heard a voice that spoke to their very souls and said 'Thou art the man'."

But what was Geoffrey's message? What did the voice say? Characteristically, it was Temple who in aftertimes, when the emotion aroused by Geoffrey's death had long calmed down, set himself the task of sorting out into lucid order the main elements of it. There were, Temple considered, three such elements. They concerned Geoffrey's ideas of Society, of the Church, and of God. But before outlining any of them Temple made two important points. In the early twenties, Geoffrey's attraction was that of an oddity living on a wartime reputation. It generally required, however, only a very short contact with him to find, behind the eccentricity, behind what a later age would have called his gimmicks—and these diminished with time—a hunger and thirst after righteousness which compelled respect. Geoffrey was also, Temple considered, a student and thinker who knew what he was talking about, and took immense pains to know.

As to his ideas of society, it was inevitable, given the conditions of the twenties, to look first for the road to social justice through changes in the economic order. This might be called, perhaps, the political phase of his thinking. He never entirely abandoned it. The whole shape of the West's acquisitive society he was condemning long before it had become fashionable, not to say safe, to do so on Christian grounds. His voice inveighed against 'our dirthy money' and its power, or stated that the only grounds for any sense of social superiority—if indeed such existed—lay in the fact of superior services to the community. He loathed our acquisitive society; he feared it; found repulsive to live with all those status-symbols based on inequalities of possession, whether of goods or power, which most of us accept as part of the natural order. He could be anguished at being called 'sir' and having his bag carried, not because he deserved the title or was incapable of carrying the bag, but because he maybe for once looked good for a tip. Such sensitivity can appear absurd. Maybe it is absurd. But it is part of the price, part of the process, of seeing things as they are, and life as it is from the uncomfortable standpoint of divine justice.

Such, then, was the first stage in the development of his philosophy of society. But as time passed its economic and political emphasis merged into something much deeper as he came to feel that society could never be changed until the men making it were changed. The operative word here is 'feel'. Many have maintained the basic premise—that inner change must precede outward reform. The difference here was the intensity of personal realisation with which the truth gripped Geoffrey as the numbers increased of the men and women who came to him, to show him their sores and to seek, never in vain, his comfort and advice. Thus it was his ministry to countless individuals which saved him from the fate of the doctrinaire, which is too often to theorise without first-hand knowledge of the instruments by which, and by which alone, the theories may be turned into practice.

So Geoffrey's great brown eyes grew sadder as the years passed, and the full truth about human-nature seemed to stand revealed. Any just order of society would, it seemed, be a long time a-coming, even if it ever arrived at all, if its architects and subsequent inhabitants had to be these extraordinary, unpredictable, neurosis-ridden, vicious, dangerous, loving and pathetic creatures, men and women, with their inconvenient habits of hating and loving each other, of sinking to surprising depths and rising to astonishing heights. Inevitably it becomes difficult, as Geoffrey discovered, to build too many hopes on any blue-print for human society, which leave out of account the guilt-ridden, the sexually deranged, the power-hungry, the alcoholic, the chronically lonely, the incurably ill, the snob, the poseur, the man with a criminal record and bright smile—in other words the whole lamentable, heart-breaking yet strangely heart-warming procession of suffering humanity.

Thus the emphasis of Geoffrey's interests passed from the outer to the inner condition of man as realisation came to him that, while, to quote Temple: "Economic conditions are among the forces moulding the moral tendencies of those who are subjected to them; far more deeply true is it that those conditions themselves are rooted in a moral state and outlook, which must therefore be the first object of attack."[1]

That last word is perhaps unfortunate as suggestive of some brisk frontal assault upon the difficulties arising from human nature's nature. Such was far from Geoffrey's thinking. Like many another, he came to see that, while human relationships were critical to any human future, their problems were not really soluble on the human level. The only destination for the procession of humanity, carrying its halt and its lame, was the foot of the Cross. So the Church came to be for Geoffrey, with all its faults and monstrous inadequacies, the hope of the world because it was the repository and the guardian of a faith which, he came more and more to feel, alone seemed to make any sense of life.

So the Church was for him the place where sacred and secular were mysteriously intermingled. If all material phenomena were for Geoffrey expressions of spirit, he was equally suspicious of anything spiritual which appeared to have no material counterpart. Temple was especially illuminating at this point. Thus, writing of Geoffrey's Eucharistic teaching: "He held the full catholic doctrine—Real Presence, Sacrifice, Communion. We take the Bread (so he taught us) and offer it, that it may be to us the very Body of Love. But while most catholic doctrine lays its stress on

[1] G. A. Studdert Kennedy: By His Friends.

what the Bread becomes to us, he laid equal stress on what it was to begin with, which enables it to become that other and greater thing. Bread is the common food of men; but it is first the fruit of man's labour . . . So the Eucharist is the focus, the gathering into a single spiritual act, of all the meaning of human life, all the aspiration towards the perfected civilisation."[1]

As was noted earlier, this aspect of Geoffrey's teaching seemed to have particular appeal for Temple, and is re-echoed in certain of his own. It was at any rate representative of Geoffrey's thinking upon the Church, upon the whole sacramental view of things, not indeed as they are, but as they could be. The Church, in short, was a society in which love was at work, and with love comes understanding and forgiveness. As to the Church on its human level, as it appears from outside in the here and now, Geoffrey never seemed as concerned as some of his contemporaries about its inadequacies. True, he played his part in *Life and Liberty*; but there is no equivalent in his writing of Sheppard's *Impatience of a Parson*. He was concerned with larger, more fundamental concepts. The organisation of the body whereby those concepts had to be mediated to the world was not a primary concern of his at any time. Always a great Christian, necessarily a churchman, he was never an ecclesiastic.

Last of all, because basic to all, was his conception of God. A great stretch of experience separated the Geoffrey who died in that Liverpool vicarage from the ingenuous, newly-posted padre who had once been moved to such furious thought by the simple question of a wounded man in an Amiens hospital; 'what is God like?' He never really ceased from developing his answer. Nor, let it be said, did he shrink

[1] ibid.

from the possibility that God did not exist. This was, in fact, the last ditch which he knew so well, where he had stood often. It was the place where the appalling possibility loomed up, like some strongpoint in the old war, in the grey dawn of a scrupulously honest facing of facts, before the rum-ration of wishful thinking had got around, that the whole concept was a man-made myth. Geoffrey's very extensive psychological studies—he had been occupied with them as long ago as his teaching days—brought him nought, or at any rate little enough, for his comfort here. So he had written:

> Suppose it is not true,
> And Jesus never lived—

What he did was to pledge the whole of himself to the proposition that in fact it was true. Faith, he was never tired of saying, was a gamble. He bet his life, as he said, upon one side in life's great war. How could he be proved right? How could God be 'proved'? He must often and often have been asked this—the stock question from the crowd. The very manner of his reply, in one of the best of his verses, *Faith*, echoes the give and take of the street-corner stand,

> It isn't proved, you fool, it can't be proved.
> How can you prove a victory before
> It's won? How can you prove a man who leads
> To be a leader worth the following,
> Unless you follow to the death?

And that, of course, was exactly what he did. It follows, that such ideas as he developed of the nature of God are worthy of respect because they were fought for so hard, and tested so rigorously. It further follows that those strange evidences, conveyed in many different ways which many noted—that he walked very close—too close for comfort—to a living Christ, are all the more moving. The outsize compassion, the soul-shaking sorrows, the natural affinity with the poor and the dispossessed, the anger with the money-changers, the fascination of him for certain intellectuals who from time to time, like Nicodemus, felt constrained to find out what this odd bird had to say, even his death, worn out and despairing, all had, and have, a peculiar look about them.

'The great illumination', as Temple calls it, which came to Geoffrey in his search for an answer to the question put to him in the hospital at Amiens, was that God is personally involved with the sufferings of mankind. That was his master-theme always. And if that has not been made clear already in these pages then they have failed badly to tell their tale. He was groping for it when a young man. He worked his way to it through the war and afterwards. God was transcendant, certainly; He was indeed 'the kingdom, the power, and the glory', the towers of York and Bach's *Mass in B Minor*! But He was not remote. No vague 'one above' He was not indifferent to the fate of His creation. He was immanent, pervading all things, involved in all things. And His self-identification with suffering invested that suffering with a mysterious dignity and significance. So the Cross, with an empty tomb and a risen Christ beyond, was the centre of things for Geoffrey, at the end, as at the beginning.

That end, all things considered, with its weariness and sense of failure, was a highly suitable one. It is difficult not to feel that if Geoffrey had gone on to be in any sense a 'success', as the world understands that word; the holder of dignity and position, it would somehow have done violence to that feeling about him which so many treasured so much—that he was so oddly like the Master whom he tried to serve.

That being so, it would have been a pity if he had marred the picture by appearing to climb any particular ladder, or becoming respected, or comfortable.

But it was all right. All these dangers he successfully avoided. Perhaps that was his only success. Certainly, he thought of himself as a monumental failure as he looked back over the way he had come. And this sense of failure, a little while before he died, he allowed to spill over into verse. They were among his last written words. Let them be so in this story:

It is not finished, Lord.
There is not one thing done,
There is no battle of my life,
That I have really won.
And now I come to tell thee
How I fought to fail,
My human, all too human, tale
Of weakness and futility . . .
I cannot read this writing of the years,
My eyes are full of tears,
It gets all blurred, and won't make sense,
It's full of contradictions
Like the scribblings of a child . . .
I can but hand it in, and hope
That thy great mind, which reads
The writings of so many lives,
Will understand this scrawl
And what it strives
To say—but leaves unsaid.

I cannot write it over,
The stars are coming out,
My body needs its bed.
I have no strength for more,
So it must stand or fall, dear Lord
    That's all.